# Typography: basic principles

## Influences and trends

# GRAPHIC DESIGN DIPLOMA SHOW '63

The Royal College of Art
School of Graphic Design invites you
to see the work of students who are
taking their diploma in
Graphic Design, Print Making
*(Exhibition Rd., S. Kensington SW7)*
and Television and Film Design
*(Queens Gate SW7)*
*19, 20 and 21 June. 10 am-5.30 pm*

JUNE

1963

20

21

Poster designed by Neville Malkin at the Royal College of Art, London in 1963. The sheet folded in 8 makes an invitation.

# Typography: basic principles

## Influences and trends since the 19th century

John Lewis

Reinhold Publishing Corporation New York

PUBLISHED IN GREAT BRITAIN BY STUDIO VISTA LTD
AND IN THE UNITED STATES OF AMERICA, 1964
BY REINHOLD PUBLISHING CORPORATION
SET IN 10/13PT GARAMOND
REPRINTED 1964
LIBRARY OF CONGRESS CATALOG NUMBER 64-14630
PRINTED IN THE NETHERLANDS
BY N.V. DRUKKERIJ KOCH & KNUTTEL, GOUDA

## CONTENTS



## ACKNOWLEDGEMENTS


To the Museum of Modern Art, New York for the illustrations on pages 22, 23, 25, 27, 29, 35 and 38.
To Marlborough Fine Art Limited for the reproduction of the Kurt Schwitters collage on page 32.
To Mr Geoffrey Clements and his students at the Plymouth College of Art for their typographic exercises on pages 70, 74 and 77.
To Mr Peter Blake for permission to reproduce his painting on page 43.
To Sidney Janis Gallery for permission to reproduce the Mondrian illustrations on pages 24 and 28.
To Willy Verkauf and Arthur Niggli for permission to reproduce the illustrations on pages 26, 30 and 34.
To the Principal of the Royal College of Art for the illustrations on pages 2 and 74.
To the Galerie der Spiegel for the illustrations on pages 73 and 76.
To Mr Anthony Froshaug for the specimen layouts on pages 55 and 56 and for his help in reading the manuscript of the book.
To my wife for her great help and encouragement.

Two examples of direct mail advertising for Spicers Precision Paper by Fletcher/Forbes/Gill.
These typographic designs owe much to the repetition of the word 'Precision', which appeared on each subsequent sheet. 1962.

# CHAPTER I Origins, and influences on the form of typographic communication

This is no place for a history of printing or even typefaces, a subject that has had the most penetrating and scholarly attention from Mr Stanley Morison, Daniel Berkeley Updike and many other writers[1]. Typography, however, covers more than a history of type design. It is concerned with the living material of the craft.

The typographer has to use material of the most diverse kinds for many different purposes. This material provides the basic elements by which he can express his various messages. It consists of typefaces, type rules, type ornaments and of sorts without any printing surfaces, such as spaces, leads, quadrats etc. As long as the typographer is working with type metal (as opposed to photo-setting) he has a definite modular structure to work to. This is an asset rather than a liability. The way he uses this typographic material is the subject of this book.

From the time the great Italian Renaissance printers such as Nicolas Jenson and Aldus Manutius printed their books in fine roman typefaces, there was little material difference in the appearance of typefaces or in the manner of using them, until the early years of the nineteenth century when, to serve the growing needs of commerce and advertising, the first real display letters appeared on the market. Robert Thorne at the Fann Street Foundry in Chiswell Street, London, issued the first fat faced letter in 1803. This was followed by Egyptians (Vincent Figgins 1815) and sans serifs (Blake Garnet and Co 1816).

On these basic display forms hundreds of variants were produced. It was a pretty heady experience for the printers of the day, to have at their disposal

1. *On Type Designs, Past and Present:* Stanley Morison. Benn, London.
*Four Centuries of Fine Printing:* Stanley Morison. Benn, London.
*Printing Types:* D. B. Updike. Oxford.

# CHESNUT STREET THEATRE

LESSEE, - - - - JAMES QUINLAN | MUSICAL DIRECTOR, - - CH. MUELLER
STAGE MANAGER, - - - - - - - - - - J. B. ADDIS

**PRICES OF ADMISSION:**

| | |
|---|---|
| Dress Circle and Parquet..............50 Cents | Second Tier and Family Circle.......25 Cents |
| Third Tier..................................25 Cents | Private Boxes, holding 12 Persons, 9 Dollars |
| Proscenium Boxes........................5 Dollars | Single Seats in Private Boxes.........75 Cents |
| Orchestra Seats...........................75 Cents | |

Doors open at half past 7 o'clock. Curtain will rise at 8 o'clock precisely.

BOX OFFICE OPEN FROM HALF-PAST 9 O'CLOCK, A. M. UNTIL 4 O'CLOCK, P. M.

# SUMMER SEASON

# PLEASING ENTERTAINMENTS!

# OPERATIC GEMS

AND

# GENTEEL COMEDIES

LAST NIGHT OF THE ENGAGEMENT OF

# SIGN'R STRINI

THE CELEBRATED PRIMO BASSO,

# MRS. ADA KING,

The Favorite Vocalist and Actress, and

# MR. EDWARD WARDEN

Who will this Evening appear in a variety of Choice Selections.

## SATURDAY EVENING, June 17, 1854

The Performance will commence with the Amusing Comedietta entitled

# THE SECRET

| | |
|---|---|
| Thomas..........Mr. CLARKE | Drunken Porter..........Mr. DEERING |
| Dupuis..........Mr. STEARNS | Angelica..........Miss WILSON |
| Valere..........Mr. ALLEN | |

MRS. DUPUIS, - - - - - - - MRS. ADA KING

After which, CAVATINA from the Opera of Cinderella by Signor STRINI

To be followed by the petite Comedy of

# PERFECTION!

## Or, The Maid of Munster.

| | |
|---|---|
| Sir Lawrence Paragon..........Mr. CURREN | Sam..........Mr. BUTCHER |
| Charles Paragon..........Mr. STEARNS | Susan..........Mrs. ALTEMUS |

KATE O'BRIEN, with Songs, - - - - MRS. ADA KING

To which will be added the

# IRISH LION!

TIM MORE, - - - - - - - - - - - - MR. E. WARDEN

| | |
|---|---|
| Ginger..........Mr. BUTCHER | Mr. Squabbs..........Mr. CURREN |
| Wadd..........Mr. ALLEN | Mrs. Crummy..........Miss WILSON |
| Captain Dixon..........Mr. STEARNS | Miss Echo..........Miss FORRESTER |
| Puffy..........Mr. DEERING | Male and Female Visiters. |

MRS. FIZGIG, - - - [Her first appearanc ] - - - - MISS PELHAM

# MR. LYSANDER THOMPSON,

## The Celebrated Comedian,

Is Engaged, and will make his First Appearance on Monday Evening.

Brown's Steam-power Job Printing Establishment, Ledger Buildings, Philad'a

# THEATRE ROYAL, BIRMINGHAM,

UNDER THE MANAGEMENT OF MR. SIMPSON.

## LAST NIGHT BUT ONE OF THE SEASON

FOR THE

# BENEFIT

OF

# MR. WAKELIN

## MADEMOISELLE & MONSIEUR GILMER,

From Her Majesty's Theatre, Italian Opera House.

## ON THURSDAY, DEC. 16, 1847,

Will be presented Wilks's Romantic Original Drama, in 3 Acts, entitled the

# KING'S WAGER

OR,

## THE CAMP, THE COTTAGE, AND THE COURT.

**PART 1st, 1651.—THE CAMP.**

Charles the Second,..............(a Wanderer from Worcester Fight,)..............Mr. COULDOCK.
Sir Charles Sedley,...Mr. COLEMAN. Lord of Clayford,...Mr. GARDINER. Captain Tattershall,...Mr. GLYDON.

**PURITANS.**

Colonel Herbert Vane,...(Officer of the Army of Parliament,) ..Mr. BARTON.
Master Small Tap Watch and Learn,...(Landlord of the "Traveller's Rest," near Shoreham,)...Mr. W. WRIGHT.
Oyasius Proudflesh,...(a Fanatic,)...Mr. SOMERVILLE. Sergeant Smite the Proud,...Mr. ASBURY.
Corporal Peter Praying for Peace,......Mr. JACKSON. Hezekiah Humble the Foe,......Mr. BLANCHARD.
Simon Preach the Truth,...Mr. YOUNG. Goliah Great in Fight,......Mr. WALLER.
Daniel Drink Water,..................Mr. ALEXANDER.
Rosabelle of Clayford,......(beloved by Vane,)......Mrs. W. RIGNOLD. Eunice,..................Mrs. POOLE.

BETWEEN THE FIRST AND SECOND PARTS A PERIOD OF TWELVE YEARS PRESUMED TO ELAPSE.

**PARTS 2nd and 3rd, 1663.—THE COTTAGE and THE COURT.**

Charles the Second,........................(King of England,)..........................Mr. COULDOCK.
Clarendon,...(Lord High Chancellor,)...Mr. LEMMON. Butler,...(Duke of Ormond,)...Mr. FITZROBERT.
George Villiers, Duke of Buckingham,......(Master of the Horse,)......Mr. C. HORSMAN.
Sir Charles Sedley,...(the Wit,)...Mr. COLEMAN. Mirondelle,...(the Emissary of Buckingham,)...Mr. ASBURY.
Lilac Lovell,.........} the King's favourite Pages, {........Miss FRANKLAND.
Chrystal Joyce,......} {.........Miss GARDINER.
Master Peter Praying for Peace,........................(now called Prayington,)..............................Mr. JACKSON.
Samson Tybbe,......................(a Night Watchman,)......................Mr. ATKINS.
First Watchman,......................Mr. MAITLAND. Second Watchman,..............Mr. BRACEY.
Edward................(Vane's Child,)..............Miss LEMMON.
Herbert Vane,....................................(an Outcast and Wanderer,).....................................Mr. BARTON.
Duchess of Devonshire,......Miss RASTALL. Countess of Castlemaine,.......Miss ELDRED.
Miss Jennings,...Miss WILSON. Lady Frances Stuart,.........Miss GARNER.
Rosabelle...(married to Vane,)...Mrs. W. RIGNOLD. Flora,...(Maid of Honour to the Queen,)...Miss MARIAN.

# A PAS DE DEUX,

## BY MADLLE. LOUISE GILMER AND MONS. GILMER.

To conclude with the Drama of intense interest, by THOMAS ARCHER, entitled the

# CABIN BOY

OR,

## THE WHITE SLAVE.

Julian,................................(the Cabin Boy,)....................................Miss FRANKLAND.
Largacette Morand, (an old Sailor,)...Mr. GARDINER. Balandier, (a retired Dancing Master,)...Mr. ATKINS.
Henri,......................(a Lieutenant,)......................Mr. COLEMAN.
Berthaut,............................................} Colonists, {..............................Mr. SOMERVILLE.
Vincent,..............................................} {......................................Mr. BARTON.
A Judge,..................Mr. YOUNG. Jacques,............(a Pilot,)..............Mr. GLYDON.
Robert,......................Mr. MAITLAND. Sailor,..............Mr. BLANCHARD.
Jenny La Roche,..............................................(the White Slave,).........................................Miss MARIAN.
Madame Morand,..................(Largacette's Wife,)..... ...............Mrs. GARDINER.

**Tickets to be had of Mr. WAKELIN, 106, Lionel Street.**

**Lower Boxes, 3s.—Upper Boxes, 2s.—Pit, 1s.—Gal., 6d. Half-Price to the Boxes only, at 9.**

Private Box, £1 1s. The Doors will open at half-past 6, and the Performance commence precisely at 7.
The Box-Office is open from 11 till 3, where Tickets and Places may be secured.—Box Book-keeper,...Mr. YATES.
**Director of Music, and Leader of the Orchestra, .....Mr. HUBERT DU LANG.**
CHILDREN IN ARMS WILL NOT BE ADMITTED. **Stage Manager,........Mr. ADDISON.**

FREDERICK TURNER, PRINTER, SNOWHILL.

Mid-nineteenth century playbills, showing an inspired use of many different display typefaces.

this great variety of type material, after nearly three and a half centuries of plain, often rather dull, roman letters. The appearance of bills and posters, labels, letterheads, tickets and all kinds of ephemeral printing changed completely, because of the variety of size, weight and form of the typefaces at the printer's disposal. Yet book typography remained unchanged, with unchanged conventions of writing and reading. Books were still printed in the style and format that the Italians had established in the fifteenth century. They were set in debased 'moderns' or, in rare cases, in revived 'old style' letters.

The first revolt against the use of these attenuated 'modern' typefaces was made in the 1840's by the printer Whittingham at the Chiswick Press, with a revival of Caslon's old face.

A much weightier protest against this de-vitalized Post-Renaissance book typography was made by William Morris. Morris was a mediaevalist, with little sympathy for the Italian Renaissance or its art, and a qualified respect for its printing.

Morris was one of the first great figures in the modern movement of European design. A boy of seventeen at the time of the 1851 Exhibition, he was shocked at the shoddiness of the products of the Industrial Revolution. As an artist he became a member of the Pre-Raphaelite Brotherhood, the somewhat exotic group of painters, who under the leadership of Dante Gabriel Rossetti were preoccupied with what they imagined to be the ideals of the Middle Ages. The art critic, John Ruskin, writing in his *Seven Lamps of Architecture* in 1849, said that the first precepts for the artist were that he should dedicate his art to God and that 'truth in making, is making by hand, and making by hand is making with joy'. These, so the Pre-Raphaelites thought (perhaps rightly), were the two great secrets of the Middle Ages. They provided a *raison d'être* for the colossal building achievements of the late Middle Ages, and they showed a way to

PSYCHE BORNE OFF BY ZEPHYRUS, DRAWN BY EDWARD BURNE-JONES & ENGRAVED BY WILLIAM MORRIS

NOTE BY WILLIAM MORRIS ON HIS AIMS IN FOUNDING THE KELMSCOTT PRESS

I BEGAN printing books with the hope of producing some which would have a definite claim to beauty, while at the same time they should be easy to read and should not dazzle the eye, or trouble the intellect of the reader by eccentricity of form in the letters. I have always been a great admirer of the calligraphy of the Middle Ages, & of the earlier printing which took its place. As to the fifteenth-century books, I had noticed that they were always beautiful by force of the mere typography, even without the added ornament, with which many of them are so lavishly supplied. And it was the essence of my undertaking to produce books which it would be a pleasure to look upon as pieces of printing and arrangement of type. Looking at my adventure from this point of view then, I found I had to consider chiefly the following things: the paper, the form of the type, the relative spacing of the letters, the words, and the

Double-spread from *A Note by William Morris on his aims in founding the Kelmscott Press*. The illustration is by E. Burne-Jones and the border by Morris.

man's peace of mind. These were the precepts tha Morris had in mind when in 1885 he founded th Art Worker's Guild (a title evocative of the Middl Ages) which held its first exhibition in 1888. Morri had become the starting point for the twentiet century 'applied' art movement.

After a lifetime of practising – most successfully – a variety of arts and crafts including calligraphy furniture decoration, wallpaper and textile desig (at which he was a superb practitioner), in 189 Morris started the Kelmscott Press in a cottage i the Upper Mall, Hammersmith. He wrote that h began printing books with the hope of producin ledge of the technique of printing. These views were first expressed in an article by Mr. Walker in the catalogue of the exhibition of the Arts and Crafts Exhibition Society, held at the New Gallery in the autumn of 1888. As a result of many conversations, The House of the Wolfings was printed at the Chiswick Press at this time, with a special type modelled on an old Basel fount, unleaded, and with due regard to proportion in the margins. The title-page was also carefully arranged. In the following year The Roots of the Mountains was printed with the same type (except the lower case e), but with a differently proportioned page, & with shoulder-notes instead of headlines. This book was published in November, 1889, & its author declared it to be the best-looking book issued since the seventeenth century. Instead of large paper copies, which had been found unsatisfactory in the case of The House of the Wolfings, two hundred and fifty copies were printed on Whatman paper of about the same size as the paper of the ordinary copies. A small stock of this paper remained over, and in order to dispose of it seventy-five copies of the translation of the Gunnlaug Saga, which first appeared in the Fortnightly Review of January, 1869, and afterwards in Three Northern Love Stories, were printed at the Chiswick Press. The type used was a black-letter copied from one of Caxton's founts, and the initials were left blank to be rubricated by hand. Three co-

10

pies were printed on vellum. This little book was not however finished until November, 1890.

Meanwhile William Morris had resolved to design a type of his own. Immediately after The Roots of the Mountains appeared, he set to work upon it, and in December, 1889, he asked Mr. Walker to go into partnership with him as a printer. This offer was declined by Mr. Walker; but, though not concerned with the financial side of the enterprise, he was virtually a partner in the Kelmscott Press from its first beginnings to its end, and no important step was taken without his advice & approval. Indeed, the original intention was to have the books set up in Hammersmith and printed at his office in Clifford's Inn.

It was at this time that William Morris began to collect the mediæval books of which he formed so fine a library in the next six years. He had made a small collection of such books years before, but had parted with most of them, to his great regret. He now bought with the definite purpose of studying the type & methods of the early printers. Among the first books so acquired was a copy of Leonard of Arezzo's History of Florence, printed at Venice by Jacobus Rubeus in 1476, in a Roman type very similar to that of Nicholas Jenson. Parts of this book and of Jenson's Pliny of 1476 were enlarged by photography in order to bring out more clearly the characteristics of the various letters; and having mastered both their virtues and

11

Double-spread from the same book as on the opposite page showing Morris's Golden type and a complete absence of ornament.

some which would have a definite claim to beauty, and at the same time would be easy to read and not dazzle the eye nor trouble the intellect of the reader by eccentricity in the form of the letters. Morris had always been a great admirer of the calligraphy of the Middle Ages and of the early printing which took its place. He noticed that fifteenth century books were always beautiful by force of the mere typography, even without any added ornament with which many of them are so lavishly supplied. It was the essence of Morris's undertaking to produce books which it would be a pleasure to look upon as pieces of printing and arrangement of type.

This is the Golden type.
This is the Troy type.
This is the Chaucer type.

The three typefaces designed by William Morris.

His observations on layout are revealing and to the point: 'I go so far as to say that any book in which the page is properly put upon the paper, is tolerable to look at, however poor the type may be – always so long as there is no (bad) ornament which may spoil the whole thing. Any book in which the page is wrongly set on the paper, is intolerable to look at however good the type and ornaments may be.' Books, he maintained are completely satisfying even if their only ornament is the necessary and essential beauty which arises out of the fitness of a piece of craftsmanship for the use for which it is made.

His Kelmscott books, cluttered up with ornament, as they were, did not quite bear out this precept. They are curiously archaic to our eyes, and essentially pre-Renaissance in conception. His use of type, however, is of interest. Morris wanted a close textured, rich dark page.

In an attempt to get away from the grey roman letter Morris began by redrawing Jenson's beautiful typeface. He said that he wanted a letter that was pure in form, and solid without the thinning and thickening of the line which Morris thought was the essential fault of the ordinary modern type, making it difficult to read. He also wanted a type that was not compressed laterally, and he came to the conclusion that Jenson's type was the only source for a roman lower case letter.

He did not copy it servilely; in fact his roman type, especially in the lower case, tends rather more to the gothic than does Jenson's. This still did not satisfy him for he felt more and more that he must have a 'gothic' (black letter) rather than a roman fount. He set himself the task of redeeming the 'gothic' character from the charge of unreadableness, which is commonly held against it. He did, in fact, design a black letter type as readable as a roman.

All Morris's leanings were towards a revival of pre-Renaissance typography; his real interest in fine books was confined to incunabula; that is to those printed before 1500. His declared preference obviously was for those set in black letter. His adviser at the Kelmscott Press, and one of the partners in an equally famous private press, the Doves Press, was Emery Walker, a devoted admirer of Renaissance printing. All the subsequent private presses followed the lead of the Doves in their admiration for the fifteenth century Italian printers and their roman typefaces. Morris alone, amongst the typographers of this printing revival, was convinced that the answers to problems of type design and other design problems lay in the study of the work of the Middle Ages. His great interest in the value of hand made things, his obsession with materials, his peerless quality as a decorator and designer of fabrics and wallpapers, all this is admitted handsomely by his historians. The effect of his work on the Deutscher Werkbund, on Gropius and on the Bauhaus is equally acknowledged. The one thing that has been glossed over is his typography. Though he has been lauded for his printing standards, his typographic design has nearly always been dismissed as mock-mediaevalism. Yet his search for a more vital page than he could get from the grey roman types led him first to his dark version of the evenly weighted Jenson types and then to his very readable black letters.

The move from a black letter to a bold grotesque or sans serif is not so far. There is much confusion about the nomenclature of sans serif typefaces. Various typefounders have called these faces grotesques, sans surryphs, (sans serifs) and gothics, which might be a clue to their origins, for the typefounders were satisfying a commercial and social demand for a black letter some seven or eight decades before William Morris produced his black letter, a true gothic typeface. The bold grotesque is much nearer to Morris's black letter than it is to the old style roman typeface. I do not think that this is

**The Advertiser**

A Regency black letter.

SONGS BY BEN JONSON.
A SELECTION FROM THE PLAYS, MASQUES, AND POEMS, WITH THE EARLIEST KNOWN SETTINGS OF CERTAIN NUMBERS.

THE ERAGNY PRESS, THE BROOK, HAMMERSMITH, LONDON, W.

Title-page from *Songs by Ben Jonson*, designed and printed by Lucien Pissarro.

too far fetched. I would claim more for Morri (speaking purely on typographic grounds) than negative rejection of Renaissance ideals and Renais sance typography. Perhaps unknowingly, he pre pared the ground for *Die Neue Typographie*, the nev movement in typography.

In the late nineteenth century in England, ther were two art movements in some rivalry with eac other. The first, the Arts and Crafts Movement, wa inspired by Morris's views on Guild Socialism an on the need to reject the machine age of the Indus

BEN JONSON'S SONGS.
A SELECTION from THE PLAYS, MASQUES, & POEMS, WITH THE EARLIEST KNOWN MUSIC OF CERTAIN NUMBERS.

I.

SLOW, slow, fresh fount, keepe time with my salt teares;
Yet slower, yet; o faintly gentle springs:
List to the heavy part the musick beares,
Woe weepes out her division when shee sings.
Droupe hearbs, and flowres;
Fall griefe in showres;
Our beauties are not ours:
O, I could still,
Like melting snow upon some craggie hill,
Drop, drop, drop, drop,.
Since natures pride is, now, a wither'd daffodill.

'age from the same book as that illustrated opposite, howing Art Nouveau influence in the border.

trial Revolution. The second was 'Art Nouveau'.

Art Nouveau was the name given to a style of decoration; the endlessly repeated motif was an elongated, rather slack, curved line. This snake-like line can be traced in the work of the French painters such as Paul Gauguin, and also in the drooping damsels of the Pre-Raphaelites, particularly in the work of Burne-Jones and Rossetti.

Burne-Jones revealed forms based on mediaeval decorations in his illustrations to the Kelmscott *Chaucer*. They were something quite outside the

OPPOSITE
Title-page for *The Gentle Art of Making Enemies*, designed by J.McN. Whistler in 1893.

Renaissance tradition; they were to be found in th
illuminated manuscripts of the twelfth century; fo
example, in the work of the artists of the Win
chester Bible. The same kind of line also appears i
oriental art. The importation of Japanese coloure
woodcuts by dealers in Paris and London had don
much to foster an interest in Japanese interio
decoration, as well as in Japanese art.[2]

This stylization and line found its way into Ar
Nouveau. It appeared in Impressionist paintings a
well; and in the work of an artist such as Whistle
where both these aspects can be found. The famou
*Nocturne* in the Tate Gallery, showing old Batterse
Bridge, might be a composition by Hokusai o
Hiroshige, and yet the treatment of the painting i
Impressionist.

Whistler's typography is of more than passin
interest. The most pleasing features of Art Nouvea
are to be found here. His use of space, his asym
metric title-pages and his very careful planning o
copy on the page was not to be seen again to such a
effect until the New Movement in Typography ha
become established in Germany, at least thirt
years after *The Gentle Art of Making Enemies* wa
first published in 1890. Whistler's consistent use o
text size letters for his chapter openings and titl
pages is yet another feature that the post-Bauhau
typographers often followed.

Pleasant examples of Art Nouveau typograph
are the very charming little books produced b
Lucien Pissarro at the Eragny press in Hamme
smith; and by Charles Ricketts at the Ballantyn
press and at the Vale, his own press which he ran i
collaboration with his friend Shannon.

Of the illustrators, Aubrey Beardsley, above a
others achieved the essential quality of emptines
or was it an appreciation of the value of spac
which is so typical of this movement.

Art Nouveau was essentially a decorative mov
ment and manifested itself particularly strongly i

2. *Pioneers of Modern Design,* from William Morris to Walter Gropius: Nikolaus Pevsner. Penguin Books, Harmondsworth.

# THE GENTLE ART

OF

# MAKING ENEMIES

AS PLEASINGLY EXEMPLIFIED
IN MANY INSTANCES, WHEREIN THE SERIOUS ONES
OF THIS EARTH, CAREFULLY EXASPERATED, HAVE
BEEN PRETTILY SPURRED ON TO UNSEEMLINESS
AND INDISCRETION, WHILE OVERCOME BY AN
UNDUE SENSE OF RIGHT

LONDON MCMLIII
WILLIAM HEINEMANN LTD.

GOBLIN MARKET

She dreamed of melons, as a traveller sees
False waves in desert drouth
With shade of leaf-crowned trees,
And burns the thirstier in the sandful breeze.

She no more swept the house,
Tended the fowls or cows,
Fetched honey, kneaded cakes of wheat,
Brought water from the brook :
But sat down listless in the chimney-nook
And would not eat.

Tender

36

GOBLIN MARKET

Tender Lizzie could
not bear
To watch her sister's
cankerous care
Yet not to share.
She night and morning
Caught the goblins' cry :
" Come buy our orchard fruits,
Come buy, come buy : "—
Beside the brook, along the glen,
She heard the tramp of goblin men,
The voice and stir
Poor Laura could not hear ;
Longed to buy fruit to comfort her,
But feared to pay too dear.
She thought of Jeanie in her grave,
Who should have been a bride ;

But

37

Double-spread from *Goblin Market* by Christina Rossetti illustrated by Laurence Housman in 1893.

wrought and cast iron. The sinuous line so typi of this movement was one of the easiest forms f the blacksmith and metal worker to shape. A Nouveau soon found its way into printing. T English, the originators of the movement, so sheered off. The followers of William Morris a the Arts and Crafts movement protested violen when some continental Art Nouveau objects we on show in the Victoria and Albert Museum.

Poster for Dubonnet by Jules Chéret, drawn in 1898 with typical Art Nouveau letterforms.

JAPANESE

Ornaments

Orpington & District *
* Industrial Exhibition,

Art Nouveau typefaces c. 1890.

Viewed through the perspective of time, there seems much that is stylistically similar in the work of both these movements. They were both intermediate movements, bridging the gap between the transitional ideas of the nineteenth century and the modern movement. The Arts and Crafts members had their feet more firmly on the ground, whereas Art Nouveau was a fleeting thing, of limited appeal to the aesthetes who accepted 'art for art's sake'.

Art Nouveau and the Arts and Crafts Movement between them made possible the work of the Bauhaus. Art Nouveau bequeathed a feeling of space and asymmetry – two of the exhilarating qualities to be found in Bauhaus design and particularly Bauhaus typography. The Arts and Crafts handed down to the Bauhaus the value to the designer, of solving his problem by handling the material himself.

In English typography, the Art Nouveau movement helped to start a new free style, in complete reaction to the centred style, used until then by every compositor. (There were few designers of print then).

The purity and spaciousness of Art Nouveau was soon debased by an accumulation of printers' ornament. Art Nouveau motifs lingered on in the design of printing, until the 1920's. Some of the display typefaces produced at this time, oddly shaped though they are, have a certain vitality which may justify their periodic revival.

Art Nouveau motifs appeared in mass produced furniture for another decade, but were finally killed by the Jazz age, with a zig-zag line that derived (many times removed) from the first of the Cubist paintings.

It was killed more by the 'modernistic' movement, so painfully revealed in the design of cheap-jack electric light fittings, and in the 'commercial art' of the 1920's, than by the cold mechanistic logic of the Bauhaus, for after all it was one of the movements from which the Bauhaus developed.

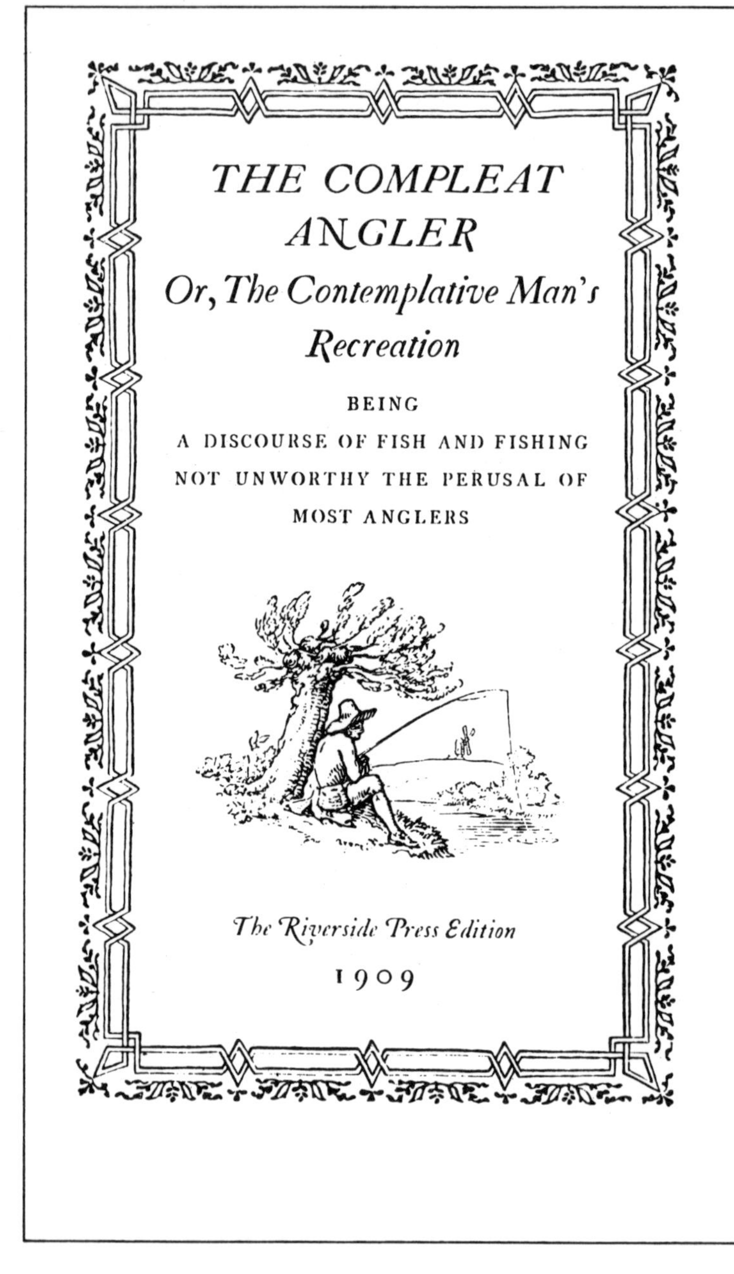

THE COMPLEAT
ANGLER
Or, The Contemplative Man's
Recreation
BEING
A DISCOURSE OF FISH AND FISHING
NOT UNWORTHY THE PERUSAL OF
MOST ANGLERS
The Riverside Press Edition
1909


Title-page for *The Compleat Angler*, designed by Bruce Rogers in 1909.

# PROSPECTUS
## & RETROSPECTUS
## of the Nonesuch Press editions

IT is now (August 1927) five months since the Nonesuch Press published a "limited edition". The length of the interval is largely due to the difficulty, which seems to be growing greater, of obtaining makings of paper in conformity to sample or specification. In colour, or thickness, or surface, or even size of sheet, paper-makers seem increasingly unable or unwilling to maintain a precise standard. Three Nonesuch books have been seriously delayed by defects in one or more of these particulars. Last year the Nonesuch Press found it necessary to destroy an entire printing of the Evelyn *Memoires* and machine the book afresh, for the faults in the paper were, unhappily, not appreciated until the book was off the press. This year two makings of French paper for *The Divine Comedy* had to be rejected, and a Dutch paper substituted; and *The*

Prospectus for the Nonesuch Press designed by Francis Meynell in 1927.

# bauhaus

zeitschrift für gestaltung • herausgeber: hannes meyer • schriftleitung: ernst kállai •
die zeitschrift erscheint vierteljährlich • bezugspreis: jährlich rmk. 4 • preis dieser nummer rmk. 1.20 •
verlag und anzeigenverwaltung: dessau, zerbster straße 16 •

2. jahrgang
1928
4

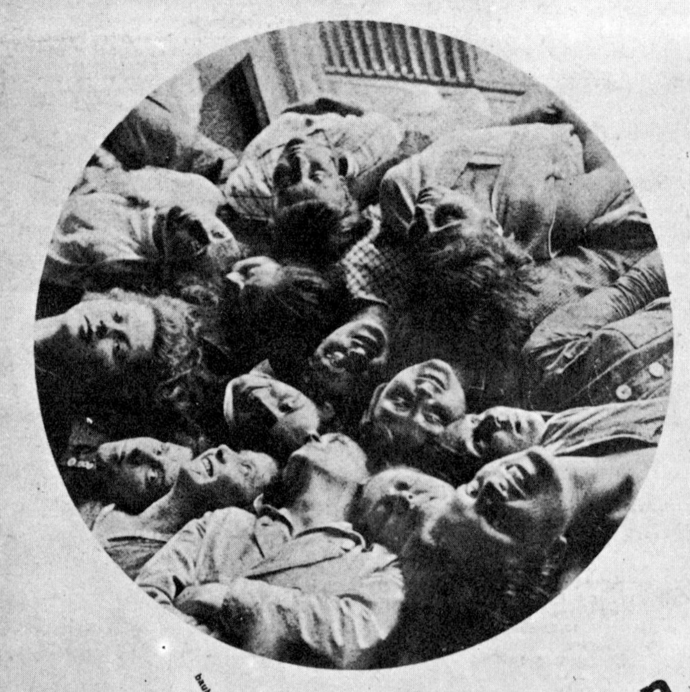

bauhausfoto lotte beese

junge menschen
kommt ans bauhaus!

POSITE
ɔver for the Bauhaus Magazine 1928. Photograph
Lotte Beese.
*e Museum of Modern Art, New York.*

*Breakfast.* Collage, crayon and oil painting by Juan Gris, 1914.
*The Museum of Modern Art, New York.*

In England, after Morris's death, the whole trend of the typography of the private presses that succeeded Kelmscott was to a revival of Renaissance typography. This was probably the last thing Morris would have wished.

Casting aside Morris's mediaevalism, the private presses based their ideas on the work of the Venetian printers and typefounders, and their successors, Garamond in Paris and Caslon in England. They re-formed their ideas, and so their printing, on Renaissance ideals. A re-birth based on a previous re-birth in the end proved a somewhat sterile thing. It resulted in two things; in fifty years of derivative typography in England and the U.S.A.; and in the deification of the old style typefaces. The typographers of this movement would have no truck with the neoclassical typefaces of Bodoni and Didot; it was the old style or nothing – and as for sans serifs . . . or the Bauhaus . . .

Morris's influence was absorbed by the German, Hermann Muthesius, who worked in England doing research on English housing, from 1896 to 1903. Deeply impressed by the work of the Arts and Crafts Movement, he inspired the foundation of the Deutscher Werkbund, mainly as a result of a public lecture, where he flayed the German industrialists for their backward-looking tendencies.

The Deutscher Werkbund was the German equivalent and the successor to our own Arts and Crafts Movement. One of the youngest of the Werkbund leaders was the architect Walter Gropius, who, in 1919 at the suggestion of the Belgian architect, Henri van der Velde, was appointed the first principal of the Bauhaus at Weimar, under the patronage of the Duke of Saxe-Weimar. This combined art and technological school was intended by Gropius to be 'a consulting centre for industry and the trades'.

Gropius at this time was serving in the army. Before the war he had established himself as a 'revolutionary' architect. His work, and so his teaching,

was based on a mixture of the Arts and Craf
Movement, German Functionalism (sachlichkei
and Expressionism. The story of the Bauhaus an
its move to Dessau in 1925, Gropius's departure i
1928 and its final closure by the Nazis in the 1930
is outside our province. The work of the Bauhau
typography workshop is very much our business.[3]

When the Bauhaus was founded, the Europea
art world was in a fair turmoil, with new movement
springing up everywhere. The most potent of thes
movements was Cubism, originating in Paris wit

3. *Bauhaus: 1919–1928:* Ed. Herbert Bayer, Walter Gropius and Ise Gropius. Museum of Modern Art New York.

The cover of *De Stijl* designed by Theo van Doesburg, 1923.
*Courtesy Sidney Janis Gallery, New York.*

| nummer | 3 |
|---|---|
| jahrgang | III |
| bezugspreis jährlich rm. | 7.20 |
| preis dieser nummer rm. | 2.00 |

bauhaus

juli-sept. 1929

vierteljahr-zeitschrift für gestaltung. herausgeber hannes meyer. schriftleitung: ernst kállai. bauhaus dessau

verlag und anzeigen-verwaltung: dessau, zerbster strasse nr. 16

typo joost schmidt

Bauhaus design by Joost Schmidt for cover of their quarterly magazine.
*The Museum of Modern Art, New York.*

the work of Picasso, Juan Gris and Braque. But there was also Futurism in Italy, Constructivism (the work of Mondrian and the Stijl group) in Holland and both Expressionism and Dadaism in Germany. All these movements had varying effects on the work of the Bauhaus for, though it was founded at least in part as a result of Morris's teaching, it was primarily a technological school. Curiously, most of the English art schools were also founded as a result of Morris's teaching and the work of the Arts and Crafts movement. These schools were soon foundering in a world of articraftiness, instead of attempting, as the Bauhaus did, to come to terms with the new age of technology with its great need for designers.

Cover for *Der Dada No. 1* designed presumably by Hausmann and Baader.

Of these movements, Cubism, Russian Constructivism, De Stijl and Dadaism had most effect on the Bauhaus typography. It is hardly necessary here to write at length on Cubism. Its origins lay in the work of the Post-Impressionists, for the Pointillism of Seurat, the colour harmonies of Gauguin and Van Gogh and Cézanne's obsession with form and structure, together had produced an analytical approach to painting that made possible the final dissection of the visible world by the Cubists, who, in their turn broke down the visual appearance of everyday objects into paintings that were quite beyond conventional observation. For example, by showing more than one view at the same time of an object, they finally destroyed the perspective vision of the Renaissance. Things would never look the same again.

The basic principles of Constructivism[4] (or Neo-Plasticism as Mondrian called it) and the origins of Dada are worth a brief digression. Mondrian's art was a logical development from Cubism and relied entirely on a rectangular grid structure, and an asymmetrical balance of primary colours and non-colours. (Grey, black and white). The exquisite equilibrium of Mondrian's work was achieved usually by placing large uncoloured areas against small coloured areas. It was an equilibrium achieved by excluding any axial symmetry. Symmetry is not merely a matter of an exact mirror image (axial

4. *Piet Mondrian:* Michael Seuphor. Abrams, New York.

Bauhaus typography, advertising building work. *The Museum of Modern Art, New York.*

BAUHÜTTE ANHALT

DESSAU
KAISERPL. 2

G. M. B. H.
TELEFON 2843

**Hoch-, Tief-, Beton-, Eisenbetonbau**
Dachdeckerei, Zimmereibetriebe, Bau- und Möbeltischlerei, Töpferei, Glaserei, Zementwaren - Fabrikation
**Kleinwohnungsbau**

ZWEIGSTELLEN :

BERNBURG
CÖTHEN
COSWIG
ZERBST

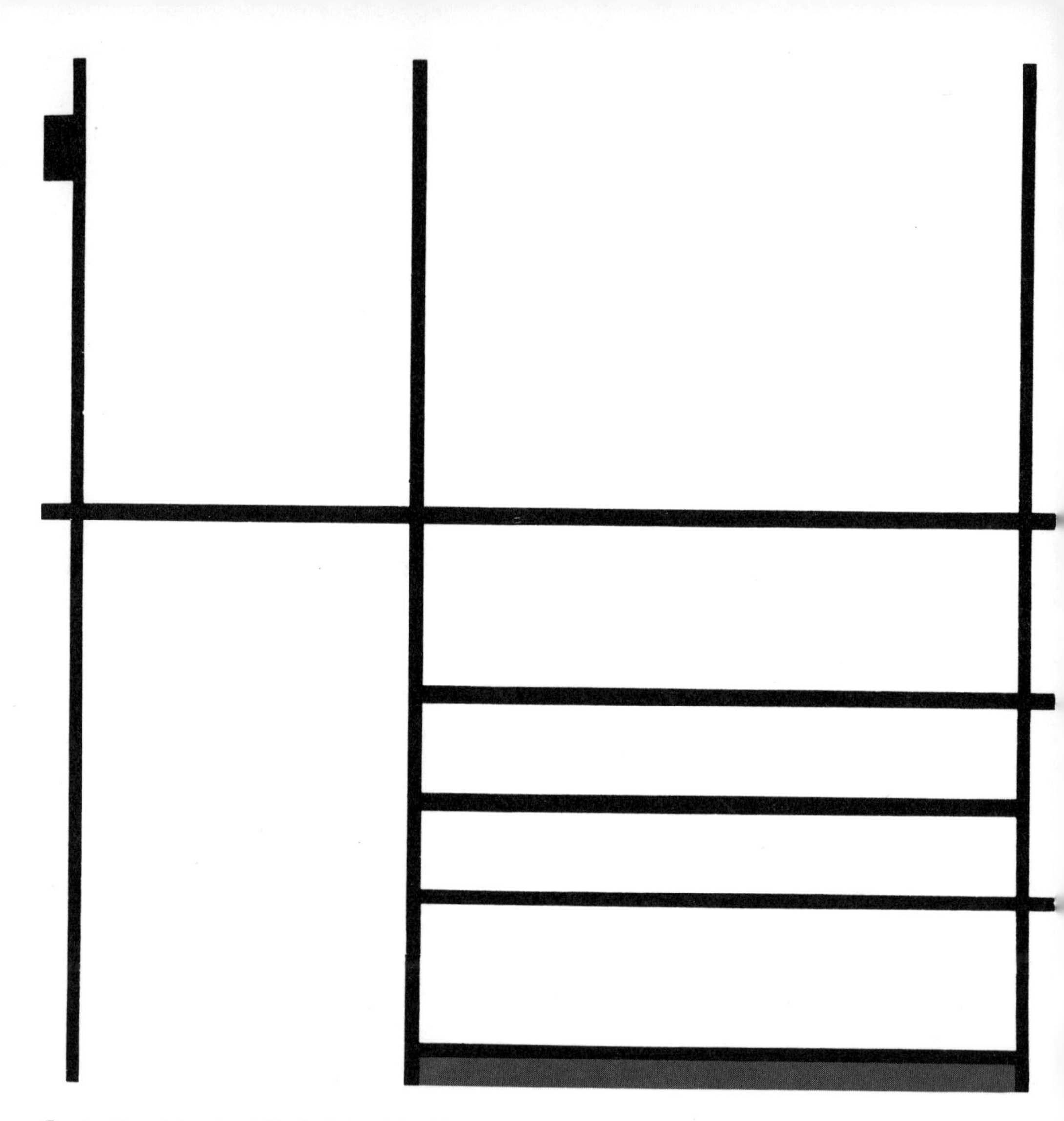

*Composition with red and black.* Painted by Piet Mondrian in 1936
*Courtesy Sidney Janis Gallery, New York.*

K 11
FAGUS
STANZMESSER
FAGUS-WERK KARL BENSCHEIDT ALFELD/LEINE


Bauhaus advertisement for a punch cutter.
*The Museum of Modern Art, New York.*

symmetry) but also of geometrical forms such as, for example, rotational symmetry. In an asymmetric layout there may often be a considerable degree of symmetry but not axial symmetry. For instance, the layout of a page of a book, which is designed as a unit, with one constant margin to the right side and a different constant margin to the left is, when viewed as a spread, perfectly symmetrical, but not axially symmetrical.

Dada was something quite different. It rejected the conventional methods and limits of painting and made use of typographic symbols, for the Dada painters regarded typography as an 'uncontaminated' medium.[5] They used the symbols in the most eccentric manner, producing a kind of childish

5. *Dada, Monograph of a Movement:* Ed. Willy Verkauf. Tiranti, London.

Back and front cover design for *Club Dada*. Berlin 1918.

anarchy. They were attempting to explode th pomposity of much Western art, letters, even civil zation. Dada provided typographers (and still does with a shot in the arm. Dada as an entirely negativ movement was inevitably self-destroying. Schwit ters, whose early work had much in common wit Dada, was by his intuitive art able to transform th anarchy of disordered collages and typography int something positive. His collages and typographica arrangements were much more than statements o anarchy. They were real works of art.[6]

After rejecting Dada, he came under the influenc of the Constructivists. He expressed many of hi ideas in the magazine *Merz* which ran for twenty four numbers from 1923 to 1932. Schwitters worke

6. *Schwitters:* Marlborough Fine Art Ltd, London.

It was the intention that each School should provide a specialised and professional training with a view to direct assistance to industry; each is in charge of a Professor who is supported by a staff of specialised teachers and craftsmen. This reorganisation, and consequent emphasis on Industrial Design, in no way implies the subordination

**The same matrices that were used to set the line in 24 point above were used here for *this paragraph in ten point.* This same 'B' set of film matrices can be used for**

St Augustine black and a modern grotesque, which have more in common than a grotesque and an old face roman.

abcdefghi
jklmnopqr
stuvwxyz
a dd

Herbert Bayer's original design for his Universal typeface, drawn in 1925.

as a typographer on the Dammerstock Exhibition at Karlsruhe under Gropius. A refugee from Nazi Germany, he eventually reached England where he lived until his death in 1944.

With Dada influences the Bauhaus typographers such as L. Moholy-Nagy, Herbert Bayer and Joost Schmidt were in a mood to reject anything.

As they rejected Renaissance concepts of architecture, with its symmetry and Palladian rules of proportion, so they rejected axial symmetry and traditional margins in their typography. They also rejected serifs and decoration, though at first the influence of Dada led them to use heavy rules and typefounders borders and squares and even stock blocks. Finally they entirely abolished the use of capital letters.

They sought to produce the ideal typeface, not based on tradition, as Aldus had done, or on human proportions as Tory had done in his letters, but repeating Dürer's (and other early experts') use of straight lines and circles, they sought a geometrically contrived alphabet. By today's standards, their work looks heavy, clumsy and perhaps rather obvious. It did not look so then, particularly in Germany where the gothic typeface was still in everyday use.

Moholy-Nagy, one of the most gifted of the Bauhaus teachers, said of typography: 'It must be clear communication in its most vivid form. Communication ought not to labour under pre-conceived aesthetic notions. Letters should never be squeezed into an arbitrary shape – like a square. A new typographic language must be created, combining elasticity, variety and a fresh approach to the materials of printing.'

Herbert Bayer, one of the instructors in the typography workshop uttered his famous dictum: 'Why should we print with two alphabets? Both a large and a small sign are not necessary to indicate a single sound. Capital A equals small a.' This was printed at the foot of the Bauhaus letterheading.

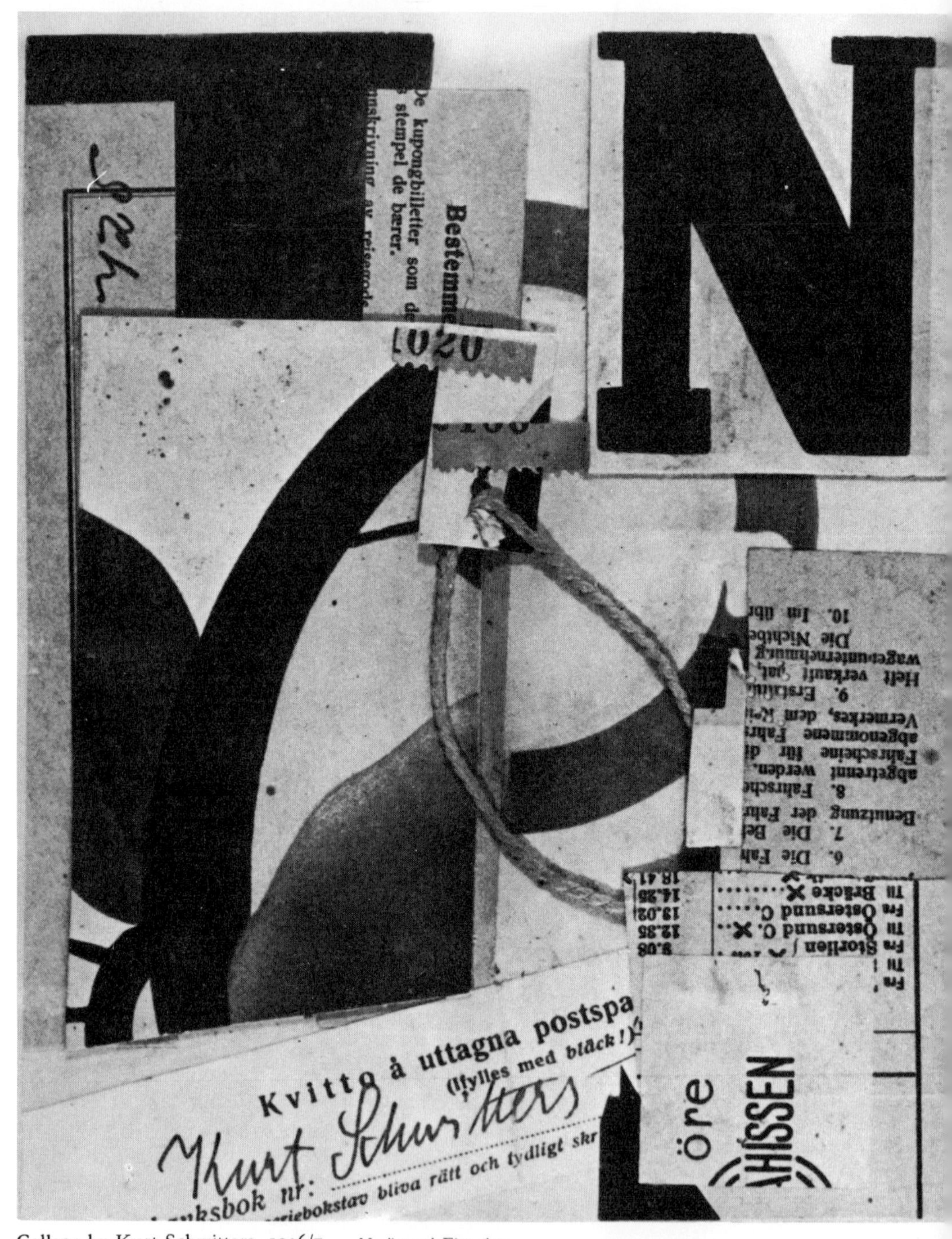


Collage by Kurt Schwitters, 1936/7. *Marlborough Fine Arts*

As a result of this, the Bauhaus began in 1925 to abandon capital letters. This immediately brought Teutonic thunder about their ears, because in German, capital letters are used for all nouns. This movement for abandoning capitals in German dates back to the philologists, such as the brothers Grimm, in the 19th century. It was supported in the 1920's by Benth-Verlag (the publishers who were later to issue the DIN standards). Germany with its use of Fraktur was ripe for a typographic revolution. The change to a dark faced grotesque was a logical solution. The roman alphabet and the old style roman typeface were only used in Germany for scientific texts, which up to the early years of the 19th century had always been written and printed in Latin.

The Bauhaus typographers brought their German standards of mathematical precision to bear, so that their new typography began to assume the appearance of a blueprint governed by precise mechanical logic. The Bauhaus books, set in sans serif, with illustrations boldly placed, set a new standard for books. The typographic style that emanates from this German work of the mid-1920's is now commonplace on both sides of the Atlantic. It has added another dimension to our methods of communication, though it was certainly not accepted immediately in the 1920's.

The feeling of revolt in the new movements of art, architecture and literature that were sweeping across Europe at this time was spreading to the world of printing. Writers like James Joyce were giving new form to the English language, but our typographers were not doing much about it. German, Russian and Hungarian typographers such as Herbert Bayer, El Lissitzky, and Moholy-Nagy were bringing a vital new emphasis to words by design, layout and the organization of space, by emphasis and their choice of typeface. Principles for this new typography were slowly being established. They

*Merz* Programme Cover designed by El Lissitzky.

called it functional typography on the assumptic that it was based on no set of formal conventions obsolete clichés (as most book printing was, ar still is) but on design planned solely for function ends. They called it Constructivist typography, b cause it was to have a logical construction and to in no way intuitive.

The basic constituents for the New Typograpl were:

Freedom from tradition;
Geometrical simplicity;
Contrast of typographical material;

OPPOSITE
Bauhaus magazine contents page, 1928.
*The Museum of Modern Art, New York.*

# 1928

2. jahrgang nr. 4
einzelheft preis rmk. 1.20


**inhalt**



## die bauhausbücher

**verlag albert langen, münchen, hubertusstr. 27**
**schriftleitung: w. gropius und l. moholy-nagy**

band 1 **walter gropius, internationale architektur** (zweite auflage) geh. **5** in leinen geb. **7** rmk.
band 2 **paul klee, pädagogisches skizzenbuch** vergriffen
band 3 **ein versuchshaus des bauhauses** vergriffen
band 4 **die bühne des bauhauses** geh. **5**, in leinen geb. **7** rmk.
band 5 **piet mondrian, neue gestaltung** vergriffen
band 6 **theo van doesburg, grundbegriffe der neuen gestaltenden kunst** vergriffen
band 7 **neue arbeiten der bauhauswerkstätten** geh. **6**, in leinen geb. **8** rmk.
band 8 **l. moholy-nagy, malerei, photographie, film** (zweite auflage) geh. **7**, in leinen geb. **9** rmk.
band 9 **w. kandinsky, punkt und linie zur fläche** (zweite auflage) geh. **15**, in leinen geb. **18** rmk.
band 10 **j. j. p. oud, holländische architektur** geh. **6**, in leinen geb. **8** rmk.

### neu erschienen ist:

band 11 **k. malewitsch, die gegenstandslose welt,** begründung und erklärung des russischen suprematismus geh. **6**, in leinen geb. **8** rmk.

### in kürze erscheinen:

band 12 **w. gropius, bauhausneubauten in dessau**
band 13 **a. gleizes, kubismus**
band 14 **l. moholy-nagy, von kunst zu leben**

**die sammlung wird fortgesetzt**


**die bauhaus-zeitschrift erscheint vierteljährlich**
bezugspreis jährlich rmk. 4.—
einzelnummer rmk. 1.20
preis dieser nummer rmk. 1.20

**abonnements bei dem verlag oder durch den buchhandel**

**verlag und anzeigenverwaltung: dessau, zerbster str. 16**
postscheckkonto: magdeburg 16662
telefon sammel-nr. 3106
für den anzeigenteil verantwortlich: hermann steffen, dessau.

**bezugs- und zahlungsbedingungen:**
abonnements haben geltung bis ende des laufenden kalenderjahres. abonnements, die 30 tage vor ablauf des laufenden kalenderjahres beim verlage schriftlich nicht gekündigt sind, gelten als um das nächste kalenderjahr verlängert. erteilte rechnungen sind so zeitig zu begleichen, daß der verlag spätestens 8 tage nach rechnungsdatum über die rechnungsbeträge verfügen kann. überfällige forderungen erhöhen sich um mahn- und inkassospesen. ausfall der zeitschriftenlieferung ohne verschulden des verlages (streik, höhere gewalt usw.) berechtigt nicht zum verlangen nach minderung des bezugspreises oder schadenersatzleistung. erfüllungsort und gerichtsstand für beide teile ist dessau.

**sendungen an die redaktion: bauhaus dessau**
für die redaktion verantwortlich: ernst kállai, dessau.
für unverlangte beiträge und rezensionsexemplare keinerlei gewähr.




**nr. 2/3 1928 der bauhauszeitschrift ist vollständig vergriffen!**

The exclusion of any ornament not functionall
necessary;

A preference for keeping within the range c
type sizes that could be machine set;

The use of photographs for illustrations;

The use of primary colours;

The acceptance of the machine age and the util
tarian purpose of typography.

The fundamentals of the New Typography we
quoted by Jan Tschichold in his *Eine Stunde Druc.
gestaltung* (1931) (Trs. by Ladislav Sutnar and re
printed in *Typography U.S.A.* 1959).

Tschichold was never connected with the Ba
haus. He started his career as a letterer and becan
a lecturer to the Munich Master Printers' School
1931. His typography was a much refined version
the rather brash early Bayer and Moholy-Nag
work. Tschichold was an intuitive designer, with
very high appreciation for the exact placing of typ
on the paper.

The New Typography brought radical new con
cepts to the whole idea of printing design. It acte
like a purge and has given us a new design languag
for tackling a thousand new design problems *f
which there was no precedent.* Problems such as th
design of photographically illustrated catalogue
Until the typographers of this new way of thinkin
gave us a way of dealing with these things, the
usually looked something like Great-Aunt-Mary
family album.

Out of all this has come unwittingly a new set
limitations. There is a certain austere prudery abo
much modern typography, as there is about muc
modern architecture and design. This puritanic
attitude would indicate that it is immoral to u
good materials, or to have wide margins. Mayb
you can have one wide margin providing all th
others are reduced to about a pica width. And on n
account must you decorate or prettify your work
which is just what Bodoni said about a hundred ar

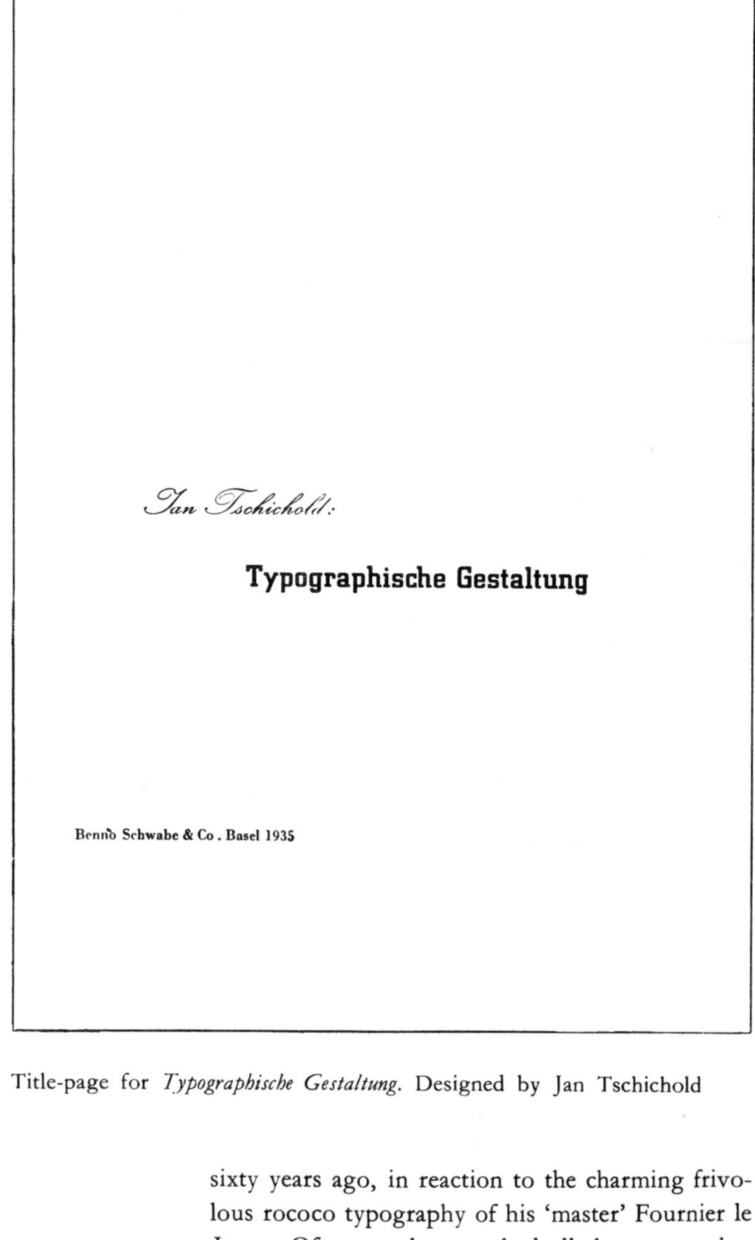

Jan Tschichold:

Typographische Gestaltung

Benno Schwabe & Co . Basel 1935

Title-page for *Typographische Gestaltung*. Designed by Jan Tschichold

sixty years ago, in reaction to the charming frivolous rococo typography of his 'master' Fournier le Jeune. Of course he preached all the more vehemently, for he was a convert to Neo-Classicism. Converts often shout the loudest.

die alte Residenzstadt der Herzöge von Anhalt besitzt zahlreiche **Bau- und Kunstwerke** vergangener Epochen,
die schöne und eigentümliche Stadtbilder schaffen!

1

Großer Markt
Seit der Gründung Dessaus am Ende des XII. Jahrhunderts bildet der Große Markt den Kern der Stadt. An den Langseiten stehen im Norden die „Buden", im Süden die Hofkammer — um 1700 von holländischen Baumeistern errichtet in den Formen des Barockklassizismus. Rechts ragt der Turm und das Dach der Schloß- und Marienkirche herüber. Rückwärts schließen die Bürgerhäuser der Zerbster Straße mit Renaissancegiebeln den Markt ab. Das Bronzedenkmal des „Alten Dessauers" ist eine Wiederholung des Schadowschen Originals in Berlin.

1

A design by Jan Tschichold for a guide book of Dessau, the second home of the Bauhaus.
*The Museum of Modern Art, New York.*

Jan Tschichold, a convert back from New Typo-graphy to a rigid classicism will now have non of the asymmetric post-Bauhaus way of thinkin Yet for many years he was the mouthpiece of th movement, and is an inspired practitioner in bot vernaculars. Tschichold's conversion in 1940 was very personal one, due to a reaction against 'milit

som den inre, ibland t.o.m. ännu något bredare. På samma sätt förhåller sig den undre marginalen till den övre. Den förra är vanligen från exakt två upp till tre gånger så bred som den senare. För dessa progressioner kan inga bestämda regler uppställas, i varje fall inga som kan tillämpas konsekvent. Satsytornas placering och sidornas uppbyggnad bestäms slutgiltigt av innermarginalens relation till övermarginalen, ett förhållande som är i hög grad svävande när det rör sig om medeltida böcker. Förhållandet 1:1,5 är visserligen vanligt men 1:1 förekommer inte heller så sällan. På det hela taget är övermarginalen vanligtvis tämligen knappt tilltagen. Undermarginalen, som ibland är tre gånger så bred som den övre, verkar bred även genom att den levande kolumntiteln ofta är skriven eller satt i övermarginalen – på tydligt avstånd från den egentliga satsytan, till vilken den då inte räknas.

Bibliotekarien Gustav Milchsack (1850–1919) har i en alltjämt läsvärd uppsats (i *Archiv für Buchgewerbe*, Leipzig 1901, häfte 8 och 10) visserligen gjort undersökningar över marginalförhållanden i medeltida handskrifter och inkunabler men överhuvud taget inte berört frågan om sidornas proportioner. En undersökning enbart av en boks marginalförhållanden är till föga gagn så länge ingenting sägs om sidornas proportioner, ty om dessa är fula kan inte ens de vackraste marginaler hjälpa upp saken.

På motstående sida: Bild 1. Proportionsskiss till en fransk handskrift från 1300-talet (Gratianus, *Decretales*). Folio, pergament. Text i mitten, kommentarer runt omkring. Sidans proportion är exakt 3:2. Progressionen är 1:1:2:3 både för de vita marginalerna och för bredden på den omgivande ramen av kommentarer. Satsytans hela bredd är exakt hälften av sidans höjd. De inre spalternas höjd är lika med satsytans hela bredd.

12

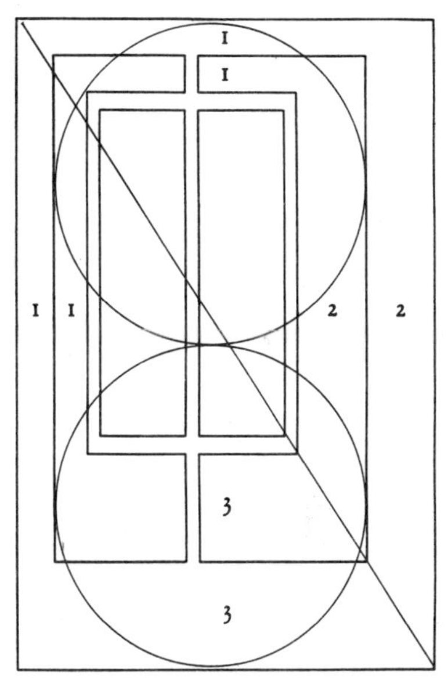


Bild 1 (se bildtext på sidan 12). Jämför bild 20.

13

Double-spread from *Designing Books* by Jan Tschichold.

ristic Nazi-minded New Typography' and his return to Renaissance typography was not a rejection of the New Typography based only on aesthetic or functional grounds. Art cannot exist in a vacuum, and though typography may be only a minor art, it cannot be divorced from outside influences.

Movements set in motion a chain of reactions so that you may all end up at the point where you started. There is not much you can do about it except to be aware of it. The day you live is today, the way you express yourself is today's way. For you cannot isolate printing from other activities; as a service industry it is vulnerable to every change of

Poster designed by E. McKnight Kauffer showing the influence of collage and Constructivist typography. c. 1935.

fashion and taste, and most vulnerable to the chan
ing face of modern art.

So, let us recapitulate; these are some of th
influences that have affected modern typograph
Cubism, Dada, De Stijl, Art Nouveau, Arts an
Crafts, the Bauhaus. The Cubists firmly establishe
that the 20th century painter had other things to d
besides providing visual likenesses of things, scen
and people; they also provided at least one approac
for modern graphic design, of which artists workin
for advertising in the 1930's made good use.

The Dadaists have given us a freedom of expre
sion and have smashed the conventions of typ
graphic communication.

Russian Constructivism was essentially a thre

dimensional art, primarily concerned with the exploration of space, not in today's inter-planetary sense, but as the fundamental element in all design. Basic design exercises with paste and paper or drinking straws and paper clips, where space can be trapped in form, derive directly from the work of the Constructivists. The most valuable contribution to typography that Constructivism gave was this appreciation of controlled space.

Mondrian and Constructivism have produced a new order, and on Mondrian's dynamically balanced grid you can reassemble the typographic chaos of the Dadaists.

Art Nouveau has offered us a stylistic freedom of decorative asymmetry.

The Arts and Crafts Movement, and particularly William Morris, have set the scene for modern industrial design. For it was Morris who identified art with everyone; who rejected Renaissance culture for the simpler world of the Middle Ages, when art was craft and the craftsman was an artist and there was joy in creative work. And it was Morris who brought the artist back into the world of industrial design, and revitalised printing by emphasising the value of craft-knowledge of media and materials.

It was also Morris who inspired the founders of the Bauhaus, whose teachers (designers and artists such as Moholy-Nagy and Paul Klee) at last began to hammer out a philosophy for modern design.

These then are the influences that I believe have fashioned the work we are doing today. The humbling thing about all this is that it is nearly a hundred years since Morris started making his prophetic utterances, it is fifty years since the first Cubist paintings were done, it is forty years since the Bauhaus was founded and nearly thirty years since the Dada movement folded up. It is not quite twenty years since Mondrian died. The creative artist (if not the successful one) is at least a generation ahead of his time.

## CHAPTER II Present day trends in typographic communication

The language of the typographer today – as always – must depend on words, and words are made up of recognisable symbols – letters. This immediately presents a problem, and perhaps a contradiction. Modern art has given the graphic artist a visual language of expression. He can cast aside the traditions of the Renaissance, spurn the ways of Palladio and Vitruvius, have nothing to do with axial symmetry and the classical proportions – and then find that he is landed with a set of Renaissance symbols – the roman and italic typefaces, in which to express his latterday thoughts. This is but one of the contradictions that our modern typographer has to face; there are hosts of others. These often belong to the job in hand; they are a kind of occupational hazard. But one thing is certain and that is that the typographer's main job is to communicate with as little interference as possible an author's or copywriter's message.

Language is not a static thing. The ever changing value of words is shown by the acceptance of foreign expressions and even slang, Transatlantic or European, into common English usage. Even more striking than this is the revitalising effect a poet can have on our tongue, by turning words topsy-turvey and inside out. If this seems far fetched, take Dylan Thomas's opening lines to his *Under Milk Wood*:

'It is Spring, moonless night in the small town, starless and bible-black, the cobble streets silent and the hunched, courters'-and-rabbits' wood limping invisible down to the sloeblack, slow, black, crowblack, fishing-boat-bobbing sea. The houses are blind as moles (though moles see fine tonight in the snouting, velvet dingles) . . .'

This may be verbal conjuring, but I think it is more, much more. Thomas, like James Joyce before him, has given the English language a new meaning, and language like visual images, needs revitalising or it becomes stale, dead.

The same need applies to the graphic arts. The painter is no longer content to work with existing conventions, which fast become clichés. He is constantly seeking new means of expression. He sets the pace, the graphic designer follows. Yet in odd and different ways they can cross-fertilize each other, for in much modern, so-called Pop-Art, there is a wealth of typographic symbols.

The tension provided by the conflict that lies between the visual impact of design and the literary

*'Pop Art'*. Painting by Peter Blake used for the back cover of the periodical *Motif*, 1963.

sense is the problem always facing the typographer and, if he is willing to accept it, always challenging him to seek new solutions. Here is his salvation. Inevitably he is a creature of his time and is influenced by the thoughts, tastes, fashions and manners of his day. Within that framework of conflicting restrictions, he has to solve his problem. If he accepts the fact that 'the seeds of the solution of any problem lie within the problem itself' he will be on the way to solving it. But the way he solves it in 1975 or 1985 will not be the same as today.

Your successful typographer can move in more than one channel of taste and fashion. He can, in the most modern idiom, be completely self-effacing. Such a one is the Swiss typographer Max Bill; such typography is typical of the Swiss. In the hands of a designer like Max Bill, it is completely satisfying; in the hands of others less gifted, it often attains an immaculate dullness. Or else he can be a complete

Double-spread from *Sophie Taeuber-Arp*, designed by Max Bill, 1948.

Sculpture en bois tourné
1937
hauteur 33

**Die letzten neun Zeichnungen von Sophie Taeuber-Arp**
von Hugo Debrunner

Im Freundeskreis erweckte das letzte Blatt der Schwarzweißfolge, die 1943 aus dem Nachlaß der unter tragischen Umständen verstorbenen Künstlerin Sophie Taeuber-Arp erschienen ist, seltsame Ahnungen und Gedanken. Gleicht diese dunkle, scharfgeschnittene Silhouette nicht einem Kahn mit hochgezogenem Segel? Deutet dieses letzte Bildvermächtnis nicht auf das Motiv einer Überfahrt hin, weg von dem diesseitigen Leben, einer jenseitigen Ferne zu?

Als ich das schmale Bändchen mit den neun Zeichnungen das erste Mal in den Händen hielt, Bild um Bild darin durchging, so wie man sein Ohr einer aus unbekannter Quelle zuströmenden Melodie öffnet, da sahen mich alle diese abstrakten Figuren wie fremde Runen stumm, doch eindringlich als eine geheime Abschiedsbotschaft an. Noch wußte ich damals nicht, daß diese Bilderfolge innerhalb weniger Tage, drei Wochen vor dem Hinschied der Künstlerin, aus stiller Versenkung heraus als ein einheitlich und unbewußt ablaufender Vorgang entstanden war. Immer und immer wieder mußte ich darauf zurückgreifen, ihre mögliche Bedeutung erwägen. Von der reinen Größe und hierarchischen Wucht eines gesetzmäßig sich vollendenden Schicksals fühlte ich mich suggestiv angesprochen.

Die drei ersten Zeichnungen heben mit dem Motiv einer vierfach ausstrahlenden Doppelsonne an. Ein von Gegensatzspannungen erfülltes Zwillingsgestirn steht in der Mitte. Die Hauptringe brechen jeweils meist nach oben hin auseinander. Der vollere Kreis sinkt dunkelbefrachtet zur Tiefe. Kleinere Segmente bilden eine Dreiergruppe. Das am weitesten aus dem Zentrum geworfene Stück liegt jedesmal links, auf der Seite des Herzens, des Gefühls, des Unbewußten, der Seite, die in den Mythen und Weissagungen der Völker als Symbol des Weiblichen, oft auch als die unheilbringende Richtung gilt. Nach links also wird das Einzelstück hinausgeschleudert, von dorther wie magisch angezogen, in eine einsame Stellung gedrängt.

In der zweiten Zeichnung, bei der sich das Schwarz zur empfangenden Schale formt, bildet das nach oben abgesprengte Kreissegment mit den in der Mitte in Unruhe geratenen Formen annähernd ein großes Fragezeichen, das sich in ein helles Licht emporschlängelt. Die Dreizahl der aus dem Umbruch entstandenen Fragmente erscheint dem Zei-

extrovert, a neo-Dadaist, tearing his words apart, setting half his message in six point and the other half in 8-line wood letters. His message, if he is successful, comes over like a slap from a wet towel; the other soothes one, graciously, perhaps to sleep.

The inheritance of the Renaissance book printer's respect for the grey page has become a millstone of grey granite round the neck of the book typographer. The first designer-printer to find this glaucous book page intolerable was, as we have already seen, William Morris.

The book typographer today, of course, has a mountain of tradition to climb over before he can produce books that reflect the character of this age and not that of 16th century Italy and France. The first obstacle is the typeface itself.

A sans serif might seem to be the obvious choice. The argument waged so hotly by the traditionalists against the sans serif typeface, is that it is not as readable as the old style seriffed letter. In the conventional layout and with twelve words to the line, it is not. But is that the right format, and the right line length for this day and age? This is at least debateable. The average line in newspapers, tabloid or otherwise, is five to seven words. This is a line that can be taken in at a gulp, or at least at one glance. After all, we do not read by letters or even words, but by groups of words. So if the line is short enough for one-glance reading, I have no doubt that a sans, and a bold one at that, would be just as readable. This opens up exciting possibilities, but what form should the sans take?

Aabcdefghijkl

Gill Sans designed by Eric Gill in 1928.

San Francisco

Futura designed by Paul Renner in 1928.

Equal working

Grotesque 215. A re-drawing of a nineteenth century typeface.

The three basic letterforms that sans serif alphabet follow are, firstly the compass and the set square sort such as Rudolf Koch's Cable, and Paul Renner' Futura or A.T.F's Spartan, which is very similar secondly the Renaissance style letters that gave thei proportions to Gill Sans; and lastly the grotesque or gothics (as some of them are called) which ar closer in some ways to the black letter than to th normal roman. And today the concensus of opinio would come down fairly heavily on the side of th grotesques. The 'compass and set square' school o thought is thoroughly discredited, if for no othe reason, because of the ambiguity of many of th letterforms, such as the lower case 'a' with it resemblance to an 'o'. (Alternative sorts are availabl in some founts for the small 'a').

The classical form used by Eric Gill for his larg family of sans serifs, though widely applauded at th time of its production, is not a satisfying form Gill's own comment, when being complimented o these sans serif letters said: 'Yes, but how muc nicer if they had had serifs'. Also, like so many o Gill's typefaces (Perpetua is an example) the letter do not combine closely enough into words, thu ignoring Morris's first principles that the face of th letter should be as nearly conterminous with th body as possible, in order to avoid undue white between the letters. This is to some extent, a inherent fault in mechanical typesetting. The clas sical Gill Sans (Series 262) in normal text settin sizes, looks like an impoverished relation to Gill' roman typefaces, Perpetua or Jubilee.

And so we are left with the grotesques. Thes types are based on a series of typefaces first cut i England in the 1830's and later in Germany an America. The first sans serif (capitals only) wa actually shown by the Caslon Letter Foundry i 1816 and there called 'Two-line English Egyptian' These types were usually called grotesques in Eng land and gothics in America.

univers

**univers**

**univers**

Three weights of Univers designed by Adrian Frutiger.

Stephenson Blake, Caslon's successors, expressed some individuality in the 1850's by calling them 'sans surryphs'.

The early grotesques were as weighty as black letter until Caslon showed a variety of weights in their specimen book of 1854. Today we have a wide variety to choose from. For text uses, Debergny & Peignot's Univers designed by Adrian Frutiger, now marketed by A.T.F. in America and by the Monotype Corporation in England, is the most thorough attempt to produce a related series of sans serif letters since Eric Gill's sans in the 1930's. Univers (American Type Founders version) has twenty-one different series. Monotype is limited to four different weights. The small sizes of the lighter weights are uniquely readable. This is partly due to the rather expanded form of these letters, which are wider in set than the grotesques most commonly used for text setting in Britain today (Mono. 126, 215 & 216).

For display use, there is today a wide range of grotesques available, ranging from very condensed letters to bold, wide and fat letters. Obviously sans serif requirements for either text or display use are very adequately catered for. Whether sans serif typefaces are the ultimate answer to text setting is of course more than debateable. Reading habits die hard and, with nearly five hundred years of unbroken use of the roman typeface, it is clear that the serifed letter may still have plenty of life in it. Letters are after all recognition symbols and if in a well designed letter, a serif adds to the recognition value, it is earning its keep. It is a point for discussion as to whether the serif does aid letter recognition, but it is certainly an aid to word or line reading. Whether or not we have yet attained any completely satisfactory seriffed typefaces for modern offset printing conditions is open to doubt. The conclusion must be that there is more than one way of typographic communication and that there is room for more than one style of typeface.

For instance, the modern newspaper, in a roug
and ready manner, has forged a fairly readable wa
of presenting its news. With all its faults of layout
setting and typefaces, it avoids the besetting si
of the purist, whether he is a traditionalist or
modernist, that is the absolute crushing boredom o
monotonous attention to precepts, precedents an
rules.

As for the alternatives to grotesques, I woul
suggest certain of the revised neo-classical or s
called 'modern' typefaces for ephemeral printing.
think these are often more appropriate than the ol
style letters.

Of the Monotype faces, Modern No. 1, Series 7,
revised Miller and Richard face which has lon
been in Monotype's repertoire, is a clear, fairly wide
most readable typeface with excellent numerals. I
has a large x-height and is cast in very small size
(Cambridge University Press use it for a wide variet
of mathematical works). Ehrhardt, based on th
types used in the Ehrhardt foundry in Leipzig, i
another useful face with a large x-height, is econo
mical in set and excellent on art paper. Walbaum,
revived German typeface originally produced in th
early nineteenth century at Weimar is a little way
ward in appearance, but has, of all the 'modern
faces probably the most charm, particularly in large
sizes. It also has a very effective italic. From Lino
type, I like Caledonia. This neo-classical face wa
designed by W. A. Dwiggins and is based on th
beautiful type that William Martin cut for Willia
Bulmer round about 1790. For unaffected clarit
the Ionics and Century Schoolbook are most valu
able.

For straight book work, old style faces such a
Bembo, Caslon or Garamond or transitional face
such as Baskerville and Fournier will continue i
use for many a day yet and no doubt new generatio
of designers will find new ways of using them. Th
text is set in 9/11 pt Garamond.

abCenturydefg
qrSchoolbook

entury Schoolbook

It is not difficult to lay down certain principles for the typography of books. To establish principles for typographic display is a very different matter, since display covers such a multiplicity of typographic uses ranging from every kind of advertising activity on hoarding, billboard, newspaper or television screen, to labels and all kinds of packaging, to letterheads and all sorts of stationery, to, in fact, every kind of ephemeral use. The importance of conveying the sense of any message is clear enough, but there are many other limitations and factors to consider.

The first factor is the typeface. What typeface should one use? Is there any yardstick to help one judge whether to set a letterhead in a fifteenth century Venetian or a twentieth century grotesque. At least one question one can raise is, is a letter A or B or C designed in Venice in 1468 the right A or B or C for today? You can argue it either way, but one thing is certain and that is, if Nicholas Jenson or Francesco Griffo or any of the great writing masters such as Arrighi or Tagliente were alive today the letter forms they designed for newspaper or poster hoarding would probably look very different from the ones they actually produced in the fifteenth or sixteenth centuries.

It is, I think, worth looking a little more closely at some of the occasions when display typography is needed, to see if, at least for specific uses, there are any valid principles which one can usefully follow.

## RULES FOR DISPLAY

Display typography means any kind of typesetting which is meant to catch the eye, whether it is on poster hoarding, newspaper headline, television screen, package or label. The rules of clarity and legibility that one follows for text setting may not necessarily apply for display work.

In any kind of advertising, the eye of the reader

has to be caught, intrigued and cajoled into readi
the copy. I would think that any typographic tri
is justified. Beautiful typography has no place he
Ugliness is a perfectly permissable feature of su
typography. Anyhow, who is to say what ugline
is? Though it may be an arch misconception to s
that function is beauty, there is no reason to suppo
that ugliness cannot most functionally serve t
needs of advertising – so much so that it perha
ceases to be ugly! The conservative printers of t
early nineteenth century reviled the new heavy f
faced letters of Thorne and Figgins which were
much more effective for bills and posters than t
roman typefaces. Today we regard those poste
with affectionate awe. The same reaction is produc
by Constructivist typography, the foundation of a
good modern display work. Ugliness is often a ter
for the unfamiliar. I would suggest that one shou
balance the anarchy of Dada against the orderline
of Constructivism. In other words, keep the obje
of the exercise always in view, but remember tha
in such typography, fashion may be a controlli
feature. Fashion is a very real thing. It is somethi
in the air, affecting clothes, furnishing, house
motor cars and every kind of design. It is impossib
to disregard it.

METHOD OF WORKING

The essence of any typographic layout is the sen
of the words. Once that has been established, the
are other factors of equilibrium and tension. T
traditional arrangements of perfect axial symmet
may still serve much typographic bookwork. T
double-page spread, optically balanced, can still
the most satisfactory layout for book pages. Whe
however, visual excitement is wanted, a rejection
symmetry is almost a necessity.

In designing any piece of print which has mo
than one page, it is possible to build up a structu
based on the position of the various elements th
appear in different pages. For example, in the la

out of a periodical, it is probably better to design from the inside to the outside; that is, first take a full text page and draw out the margins and the positions of the type, folios etc, then add the position of a chapter or article opening. On those beginnings build up every possible, or at least likely, permutation of illustration. This structure will now begin to look like a grid-iron, or at least a bit like a Mondrian painting. Into this grid you can now, unerringly, place any other element including details of contents, title pages, covers etc.

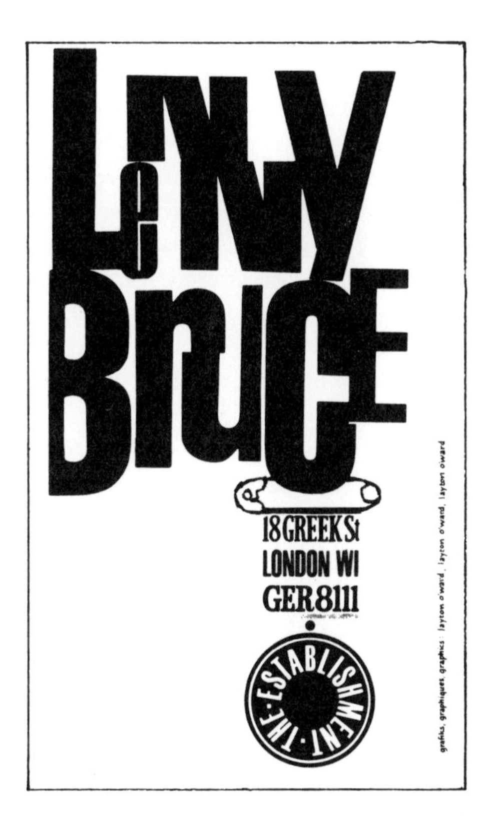


Advertising card for Lenny Bruce at The Establishment, 1963.

The primary job of the typographer is commun cation, though today the advertising world ma ask rather more of him than this. Our job is basicall to communicate by typographic means. To do th we start with copy . . . words, an author's manu script . . . a copywriter's scribble on a memo pad.

In every problem lie the fundamentals of it solution. So, read the copy. For the moment, let u forget the difficulties and limitations of book typo graphy and concentrate on copy that can be en compassed by broadsheet or advertisement space The form of any piece of typography must b dictated by the words. So, read your copy; digest it understand it, then, within the area or the pro portions of your advertisement or paper size, writ it out. Do not worry about type forms. Just writ it out, in pen or pencil or what ever comes easiest t you. I normally do my preliminary scribbles to very small size in fountain pen. It is the content I ar concerned with. The form can keep changing bu not the sense. Once I have produced what I thin is the most rational arrangement of my message I will then write it out again very freely in a so pencil to the right paper size. Only then will I star worrying about the sizes and the kinds of typefac I want to use.

A lot of nonsense has been talked about the appro priate use of typefaces for certain kinds of job I was once asked to design a type book on thi principle. You know the kind of thing: delicate pretty little scripts for cosmetic advertisements classical, formal and eminently respectable roma faces for Banking Houses and Money Lenders black letter for Church and Law, big chunky san for Heavy Engineering. It was only after I had designed about twenty of these examples that I found I could change their typefaces round at will and with ever increasing effect!

Limitations are an asset. The typographer working in an agency has the bewildering freedom of the large typesetting house, which carries everything. Working for the average publisher or printer, he may find much more limiting factors. The printer may only carry four or five different suitable text faces and of those, perhaps only one or two in the exact size he wishes to use. It is surprising what a help this is.

Let us suppose you have decided to use a grotesque, say Monotype series 215 and 216. You slip your typesheet under your roughly pencilled layout and match up, as near as you can, the size of type to the letters you have drawn, then rub these out and trace the types through. It is not very difficult. It is, however, worth taking great care, even infinite pains. A sensible practice is to decide on what size of type you think you will need, trace it through on to a narrow slip of paper and do this for each different line, then slip these under a clean sheet on which you have ruled out the paper and type areas. Juggle your lines about until they look right viewed through this top sheet, then retrace. NEVER try to save time pasting down these slips on top of your clean sheet. They never look right; the edges of the slips optically reduce the space between the lines, and when your layout is set, it is certain to look pathetically open.

One rule of thumb is, when in doubt about what size to set either a display or text line, set it in a smaller size than you first think may be necessary. I don't know why this should be, but it works.

When representing areas of text setting, if the layout is going straight to the printer, it is enough to outline the area; if the layout is to be shown to a client, it is as well to indicate the tone of the type area. Do this by ruling in with a soft pencil doubl lines at the x-height of each line.

The mechanics of typography are simple enough Any literate person can learn them in a week or sc After that, if he has any kind of eye, he shoul be able to produce agreeable, possibly effectiv pieces of typographic design. From then on it is matter of experience; of just plain doing it.

Jan Tschichold once said: 'simplicity of form i never poverty; it is a great virtue.' How true! Fo one doesn't have to try to be clever; if one reall understands the sense of words the rest shoul follow. If the sense is understood, the typographi styling should follow that sense, attempting only t elucidate, possibly to amplify, never to confuse th meaning. Experience is the only teacher. The soone the young typographer can gain experience, th sooner he will know what he is doing, so it is bette not to dissipate these early experiences. It is fa better to know one typeface well and even only on or two sizes of that face, than to have a dim appre ciation of a number of different faces. So, to begi with, work a face to death, so that you can find ou just what it will and will not do in different size under different circumstances and on different pape surfaces. No face is perfect for everything; certai sizes are better in one face than another. On th whole, large x-height faces like some of the Gro tesques or Times New Roman are good in sma sizes e.g., 6 point Univers 689 or 7 point Times Ne Roman. Small x-height letters with long ascende and descenders are better in larger sizes e.g., 12 poi Bembo or 13 point Perpetua.

The essence of typography lies in interpretin words, and so sense, clearly. To do this, there rather more to be considered than the choice of particular typeface and its appropriate size. Th first thing is the length of line. A readable line in book is of ten to twelve words. For approxima casting off, a word equals six characters. These s

| 24 June 1946 | | **Balance Sheet** |
|---|---|---|
| | | **Properties** (as valued by Messrs Farebrother, Ellis & Company at June 1937, or on subsequent completion, plus additions at cost) |
| | 164 838 | Freehold |
| | 3 868 404 | Leasehold (certain properties have suffered War Damage) |
| | 42 000 | Artesian Wells & Water Treatment Plant (as valued by Messrs Farebrother, Ellis & Company £49 000 less amount written off) |
| | 4 913 | Air Raid Shelters (at cost less recoveries) |
| | 128 714 | Property Suspense Account Balance (arising on Property completed and valued 1940) |
| | 89 502 | Contributions under the War Damage Acts Part I |
| | 4 298 701 | |
| | | **Mortgage Debenture Stocks** |
| 000 000 | | 5% First |
| 000 000 | | 4% First |
| 000 000 | | 4% First [1945] |
| 000 000 | | 5% 'B' |
| 1 697 669 | | |
| 1 343 835 | | Mortgages & Loans secured on specific properties |
| 3 041 504 | | Total Loan Capital |
| 78 026 | | Pr- |
| | 2 963 478 | |
| | 1 334 893 | |
| | 18 571 | Leasehold Redemption Fund *deducted* |
| | 1 316 322 | |
| | 6 567 | Furniture, Fixtures etc |
| | 48 000 | Investments in Subsidiary Companies |
| | 1 370 889 | |
| | | **Current Assets** |
| 26 905 | | Cash at Bankers & on hand |
| 20 000 | | Tax Reserve Certificates |
| 63 523 | | Debtors |
| 5 012 | | Amounts due from Subsidiary Companies |
| 9 127 | | Stocks |
| 7 527 | | Rates etc in advance |
| 132 094 | | |
| | | **Current Liabilities & Provisions** |
| 20 762 | | Accrued Interest on Mortgage Debenture Stocks, Mortgages & Loans |
| 96 481 | | Taxation on Revenue to date |
| 68 727 | | Creditors, Specific Provisions & Accrued Expenses |
| 69 148 | | Amounts due to Subsidiary Companies |
| 94 353 | | Provision for Repairs, Decoration & Maintenance |
| 349 471 | | |
| | 217 377 | **Excess of Current Liabilities & Provisions over Current Assets** |
| | 1 153 512 | **Net Balance representing Shareholdings** |
| | | **Capital fully paid** |
| | 500 000 | |
| | 100 000 | |
| | 400 775 | |
| | 1 000 775 | |
| | 152 737 | **Revenue Account Balance** |
| | 1 153 512 | |

**26 October 1946**

**Report of the Auditors to the Members**

We have audited the above Balance Sheet. We have obtained all the information & explanations we have required. In our opinion such Balance Sheet is properly drawn up so as to exhibit a true & correct view of the state of the Company's affairs according to the best of our information & the explanations given us and as shown by the books of the Company

*H N Murray & Company*
Chartered Accountants

Revenue House, 7/8 Poultry, London EC2

Layout by Anthony Froshaug for a page of accounts, drawn in red and black inks.

Alain-Fournier

Translated
by Françoise
Delisle

8pt Bodoni u/lc
set solid

# The Wanderer . Le Grand Meaulnes

Illustrated
by John
Minton
and with
an Introduction
by Bonamy
Dobrée

10pt Bodoni u/lc

Paul Elek Publishers Limited . London

10pt Bodoni u/lc

units include inter-word spaces and punctuation marks. An even more readable line is the normal column setting of a newspaper or journal, of from five to seven words. As I have already said, one tends to read not by individual letters or even words, but by groups of words. Your tabloid newspaper line can be taken in at one glance. The line in a novel has to be followed through, and then the sense picked up in the next line. If your line is long, say eleven to thirteen words, it may be difficult to pick up the succeeding line. In this case increase your inter-line spacing by leading (leads for hand setting are strips of metal 1 point, 1½ points, 2 points or 3 points thick; for machine casting the equivalent one, two or three points are cast with the types, so making the body of the type deeper).

Too large a setting can be almost as unreadable as too small a setting and, for text matter, certainly far uglier because of the inevitable unevenness of spacing between words, unless the measure is increased to include the same number of words.

LEADING

The judicious use of leading is one of the great factors in successful typographic layout. Here one is handling white space, one of the key elements in typographic design, whether it is used for leading or margins or in any other way. As simplicity is the keynote of most successful design, so in typography, the simpler the tonal contrasts in your black type, your grey areas of text setting or your white space, the better. Avoid a kind of pepper and salt mixture of these elements lest all tonal contrast be lost.

For display, particularly with grotesques or modern typefaces, the rule for leading formulated by G. B. Bodoni was to use one third of the body size. That is, for a twelve point setting, you would use a four point leading. This is far more open than one normally uses for book work and would certainly not have the approval of William Morris, who

OPPOSITE
Layout for a title-page by Anthony Froshaug with type mark-up limited to essential factors. The careful drawing of the type matter and its accurate positioning obviates the need for further instructions.

disapproved strongly of 'the modern practice of leading'. In fact, for old face types such as Bembo or Garamond that have long descenders, little leading is needed. Likewise, for short measures set in grotesques or other evenly weighted typefaces, the text usually looks better with little or no leading. If, however, one was setting twelve point Monotype Bodoni 135 to a normal book measure, a four point leading would suit it perfectly. The strong contrasts and vertical stress of this neo-classical face make it virtually unreadable unless it is leaded.

CASTING-OFF

When you have to handle more than a few lines of copy, which you can write out in type size, you have to assess very accurately, in the case of a book or a magazine article, or even a lengthy advertisement, exactly what space your printed text is going to occupy. The simplest method is to count the number of characters (including punctuation marks and inter-word spaces as characters) in an average line of manuscript, multiply this by the number of lines in a page and this figure by the number of pages in the complete manuscript. Then divide this figure by the number of characters in a specimen line of type set to the measure you propose to use. This will give you the number of printed lines. If they are too many, reduce the size of your setting, or increase your measure, or both. For very accurate casting-off of relatively short pieces of copy, such as for advertisements, it is essential to apply this proceedure to each separate paragraph, and actually to count every character.

TYPE-RULE

This is usually a twelve inch steel rule with inches and eight point measure on one side and ten point and twelve point measures on the other. The normal unit of linear measurement in typography is the twelve point em (or pica). There are twelve points in an em and approximately six ems to an inch.

LAYOUT PAD

This should be of good quality smooth Bank paper, transparent enough to see the letters on a type sheet clearly when this is slipped under a sheet of layout paper. An accurate, straight-sided drawing board, set squares and T-squares of good quality are of course necessary, as are hard and soft pencils and a soft rubber and type specimen sheets. Use a sharp H for 6 pt, a sharp HB for 12 pt and a sharp 2–4 B for display-size letters.

TYPE SPECIMENS

Without typesheets the typographer cannot usefully practice. The working typesheet should show every character in the fount and every point size. Most typefounders and typesetters will supply specimen sheets but these are mainly for publicity purposes and do not show complete founts. The ideal working sheet is that published by the Monotype Corporation Limited in collaboration with the printers Oliver Burridge and Company Limited. For sheets such as these or for the Wace or Layton typesheets one of course has to pay. These typesheets are an essential part of the stock-in-trade of any typographer.

When your layout is complete, mark it up outside the area in ink or coloured pencil, so that there is no confusion between what is to be set and what are the instructions. Put in the minimum amount of instructions, properly phrased. In printing, like any other trade, there is a language which one should follow. Even in a simple instruction for the setting of text in galley the typographer will word his instructions something like this: Set in 11/12 pt Walbaum series 374 to 24 ems.

11/12 pt means eleven point setting cast on a twelve point body, so including a one point lead. In short amounts of copy, for advertisement setting etc. it is more usual to mark the leading separately. Thus: 11 pt Walbaum 1 pt leaded. Walbaum is the name of a typeface; the series number is Monotype's designation for that particular face. A bolder version of

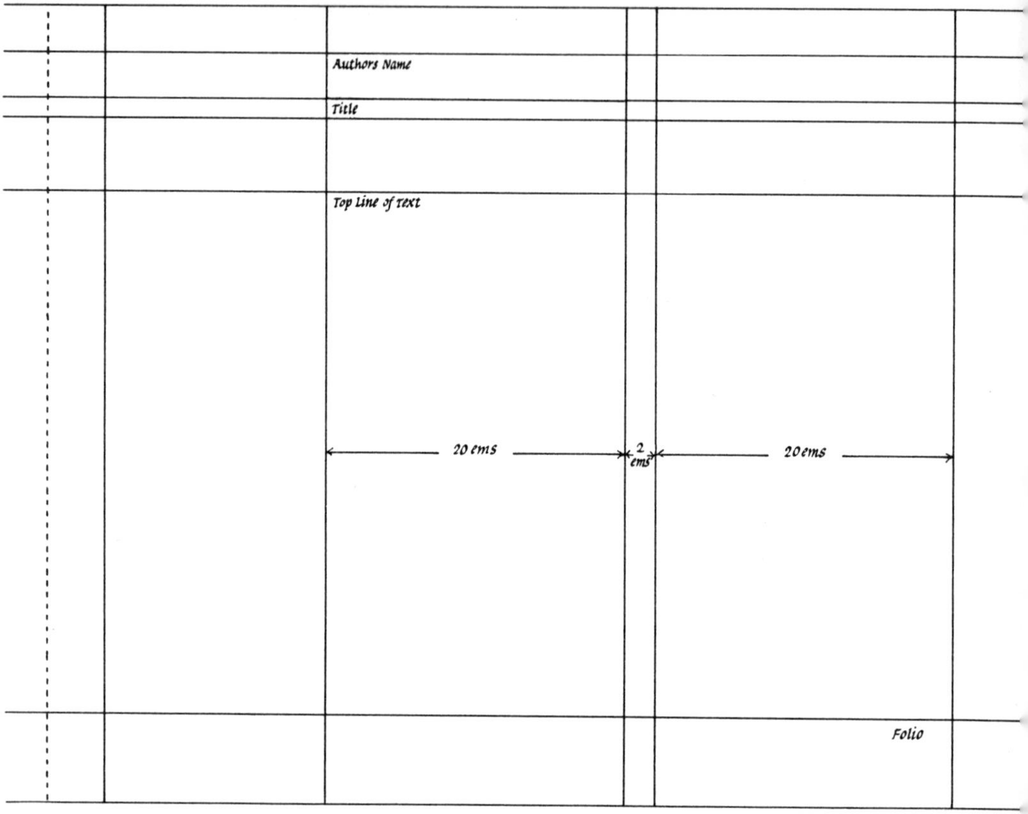

Authors Name

Title

Top Line of Text

20 ems | 2 ems | 20 ems

Folio

A simple grid for the layout of the Shell Chemical Company's magazine *Catalyst* designed by John Lewis. On this structure both left and right hand pages are laid out. The text always falls in the two right hand columns and the photographs can fill any of the rectangles shown here, though on occasions when captions are necessary and have to go below the photograph, they will be incorporated in the same area.

Walbaum has a different series number. 24 ems is the width of the line equalling four inches.

The next thing you know, you have a proof in front of you and it bears no resemblance to what you intended! Don't panic! Sit down and compare it very carefully with your layout. If it is a galley proof trim it and mount it to exact size on your layout pad so that the ruled-in margins encompass it. The visual appearance of type changes markedly when this is done. The apparent size of a display line can alter in an extraordinary manner if margins are reduced.

Check very carefully everything the printer has

**Catalyst 2** AUTUMN 1959

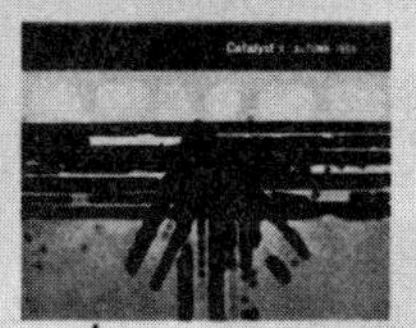

CONTENTS




ACKNOWLEDGEMENTS

The photographic cover design is by Geoffrey Ireland.

The drawings for the A.B.C.M. article are by Anthony Atkinson.

The drawings for 'The Ethylene Story' are by Derek Cousins.

The colour carpet illustration is reproduced by courtesy of The House of Perez.

Drawings for 'Italian Industrial Chemical Developments' are by Geraldine Spence.

The drawings for the article 'Watching Television for Gain' are by Jill Francksen.

Edited by D. Wolters, Public Relations Department, Shell Chemical Co. Ltd., 170 Piccadilly, W.1.

Designed by John Lewis.

Printed in England at The Curwen Press.


THE COMPANY'S TECHNICAL SERVICE LABORATORY AT EGHAM, SURREY

This reception area designed by John Diamond for the Green Park Hotel, London, creates an impression of efficient and friendly service which is what most people want today. *Photo:* Sam Lambert

10

done, mark it up where he has not followed you
copy; and mark it up where he has and it doesn'
look right. When marking up proofs of manuscript
use the customary proof correction marks. Thes
are a set of weird hieroglyphs, which printers hav
used since I don't know when. They are nov
published by the British Standards Institution.

These are the most used abbreviations:

caps – capitals  s.c. – small capitals  ital – italics
rom – roman  w.f. – wrong fount  trs – transpos
stet. – leave as printed (even if crossed out)
l.c. – lower case
u.c. – upper case
u and l.c. – upper and lower case

delete  insert

# space  ⊙ insert a full point

indent 1 em

close up  ,⋏ insert comma

?⋏ insert question mark

move line to right

move line to left

run on

Proof correction marks.

PREPARATION OF MANUSCRIPT FOR THE PRINTER

When for the first time a pile of manuscript arrive
on the typographer's desk, with a brief request t
mark it up for the printer, he may well feel awed
This, like any other job, is a matter of experience
The procedure is as follows:

1. Check to see that the manuscript is in the cor
rect order and that the pages are numbered.

2. Cast off, noting whether there are any length
quoted passages of text, which may well be se
smaller or indented; also whether there are foot
notes, which will certainly be set smaller than th
text. Decide on type sizes, measures and number c
words to the printed page.

3. Lay out specimen page spread, showing on th
left the treatment of the chapter headings and on th
right any subheadings or other peculiarites of th
text. In the case of complicated, perhaps scientifi
texts, it will probably be necessary to have at leas
three pages set to cover all the text treatments.

4. Whilst specimen pages are being set, chec
manuscript inconsistencies in use of capitals, etc., fc
literals, and mark up for any special differences c
house style. If the printer is an experienced boo
house, most details of house style can be left to him
including methods of spelling, e.g. the use of 'z' c

's' in such words as realization (Oxford) and realisation (Cambridge). If you are using a trade typesetter or a general jobbing printing house, leave nothing to chance. In a publishing house, much of this copy preparation should have been done by the editorial department. But if you are working for industry, it will probably be up to you.

5. Prepare copy for preliminary pages, including contents page, list of illustrations etc. This rarely comes with the manuscript. Any words to be set in italics mark with a single underline, those in small capitals, with a double underline and those in capitals with three underlines.

6. Notes can be placed at the foot of the page, set at least two points smaller than the text; or in the margins, if your margins are wide enough. In this case they need to be set even smaller. Or they can appear at the end of the chapter or at the end of the book. The simplest way of indicating them in the text is by way of superior figures. These are very small figures cast separate on the shoulder of the type. In the manuscript, indicate matter that is to be set smaller, by a vertical line in the margin with the setting size indicated alongside.

7. On anything to do with methods of literary style, or spelling, consult Fowler's *Modern English Usage* (Oxford), *Authors' and Printers' Dictionary* by F. Howard Collins (Oxford) or the *Oxford English Dictionary* in one or other of its forms.

## THE ECONOMICS OF TYPOGRAPHY AND PRINTING

The typographer has to concern himself with the economics of production. He should find out what the limitations of his printer, or printers are, and then work to the *limit* of those limitations. This is no bad thing. Limitations are a help rather than a hindrance, for they help a designer to channel all his efforts in one direction. For any kind of design for print, it is essential to know the maximum size of sheet that can be printed most economically for the job. In simple terms, this usually means that

OPPOSITE
Poster designed by the French artist Jacno showing a very free interpretation of a stencil typeface such as Teachest.

the more sub-divisions you can get from your sheets, the less the machining cost per page will work out. In other words, if a book you are designing can be printed 32 pages to a sheet instead of 16 or 8, it will cost less per page. This does not mean that a typographer has slavishly to follow conventional book sizes, but that he has to work within the maximum limitations of paper sizes. For example, this book's page size is $7\frac{3}{4}'' \times 6\frac{1}{2}''$, it comes out of a sheet size $28'' \times 49\frac{1}{4}''$. As it is a special making of paper no paper is wasted, though a slightly larger sheet could have gone on the machine.

It is also important to find out whether for the size of sheet you wish to use, your printer has only single colour or two-colour machines. If the latter the advantage of a second colour should be considered. The additional cost may not be very much.

There are various money-saving procedures, particularly in the reproduction of illustrations, which are rather outside the scope of this book. If half-tone or line subjects are grouped for the same reduction, you can save on block charges. If you are working for offset and can work with sufficient precision to do the make-up, that is pasting-up reproduction type pulls and bromides of illustrations in the exact position for camera, you can save a lot of money. Incidentally, letterpress printers who excel at text printing on antique papers usually have little idea of how to print a half-tone on art paper, and the same applies in the other direction!

For typesetting that has to be done on the keyboard and cast in hot metal, the fewer the sizes you use, the cheaper the job will be. The scope for example of a Monotype matrix is not inconsiderable, for it carries 225 matrices (the enlarged matrix carries 255) and offers you the following:

In roman: capital letters, small letters, small capitals, numerals, punctuation marks and ligatures.

THEATRE NATIONAL POPULAIRE

TNP

JACNO

Festival

d'Avignon

In italics: capital letters, small letters, numera
punctuation marks and ligatures.

In bold: capital letters, small letters, numera
punctuation marks and ligatures.

Designing purely within the scope of say, a
point fount, offers you a challenge that is n
difficult to meet, with the advantage that one has
constant tonal value. Make-up is rarely done on t
typesetter, for the keyboard operator is bett
employed hammering out copy. So, niceties of sp
cing, using only multiples of your text size, a
irrelevant. The make-up is done on the stone and
does not matter, from the point of view of savi
production costs, if you have asked for a 12 or
point space between lines of your copy.

In the imposition of books and periodicals, ca
should be taken in positioning illustrations th
bleed. Check this point with your printer. Likewi
in book work, where half-tone art paper illustratio
are included in a book printed on antique paper, t
to group these together, so that a section of a
paper can fall between sections of antique, or ins
them as wrap-rounds, wrapping complete sectio
Never try to insert wraps between say, pages 1 an
and 14 and 15 of a 16-page section. The handwo
involved in slitting the bolts is too costly.

The use of obscure typefaces, obtainable o
from foreign typefoundries must run you into ex
cost. It may be worth it. The use of display typefa
not carried by your printer also involves extra co
because he either has to hire matrices to cast the ty
and has to clear a case to house it, or he has to b
the type from a typefoundry or obtain type r
production proofs from a typesetter. The latter a
absurdly expensive. From these reproduction proo
line blocks will have to be made.

## FILMSETTING

Filmsetting is not exactly a new thing, for it was first patented nearly seventy years ago. In comparison with metal type, the photo-typesetter offers an unbelievable amount of freedom to the typographer. The typographer used to working for offset must have a fairly good idea of the potentialities of this two-dimensional typesetting.

When working for offset in a plant only equipped with hot metal setting, the make-up or layout man preparing copy for the camera assembles reproduction proofs, taken from normal type. This offers a fair amount of flexibility, for display type can be placed without any of the space that would have to show if one was printing from metal. The only limit to what one can do is the limit of scissors and paste

**USE OF THE IMAGE**

**USE OF THE IMAGE**

**die unentbehrlichste schrift**

**Bauersche Gießerei**

he freedom of the photographic image,
here letters can be made to abut or overlap.

This same flexibility is carried into photo-typesetting but with certain advantages. An obvious one is the greater definition, for the printed letter is much sharper than normal printed type or even type pulled on Barytra paper specially for reproduction processes. To some extent the actual thickness of the filmset letters can be controlled to suit differing paper surfaces.

Some of the filmsetters are calibrated on a point system, others work to a metric scale. This is of no little importance to the designer for he has almost

# 'Monophoto' HEADLINE BOLD

**The same matrices that were used to set the line in 24 point above were used here for *this paragraph in ten point.* This same 'B' set of film matrices can be used for any size from 8 up to 22 and 24 point.**

**FOR THE 7 AND 6 POINT SIZES, USE THE 'A' SET OF MATRICES**
**Here is a specimen of Series 595 in the *six* point size, produced with the 'A' set of matrices which can also be used for 7 pt.**

# 'Monophoto' GARAMOND

The same matrices that were used to set the line in 24 point above were used here for *this paragraph in* TEN POINT. This same 'B' set of film matrices can be used for any size from 8 up to 22 and 24 point.

FOR THE 7 AND 6 POINT SIZES, USE THE 'A' SET OF MATRICES
Here is a specimen of Series 156 in the *six* point size, produced with the 'A' set of matrices which can also be used for 7 pt.
**The related Bold is Series 201.**

For Monophoto filmsetting there are three basic film matrices; the A set is for 6 and 7 point, though it can be used for smaller sizes; the B set is for from 8 to 12 point and the C set is for sizes from 14 to 24 point.

stereo

This word could have been made from a C Monophoto matrix.

unlimited flexibility in letter size, in leading an spacing. This means he can set in 14½ point with point leading if he so wishes. With an accurate la out the bulk of the make-up can be done on th filmsetter. As a result instead of having to assemb a number of separate strips of letters, a whole pag can be exposed on one piece of film. The availabili of typefaces varies from one typesetting house t another. In theory it would seem that any typefac that is cast in hot metal could be used for phot typesetting.

A very real advantage of photo-typesetting is th sizes larger than 14 point (the normal maximum fo Monotype keyboard setting) can be set as easily small text sizes. The advantages of this method fo children's books hardly needs emphasising.

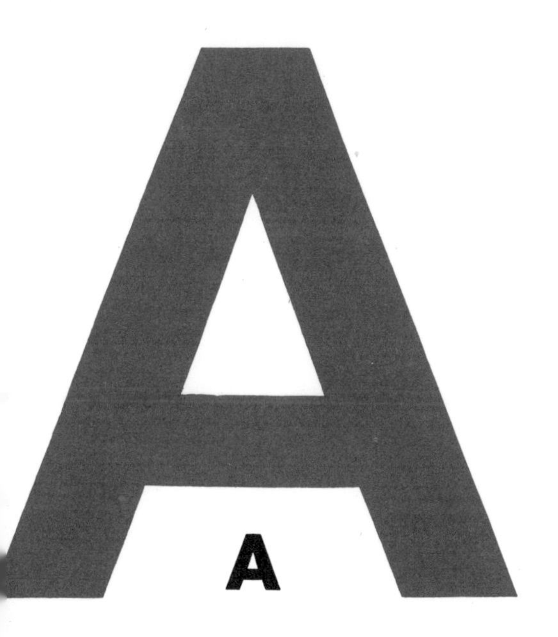


ost filmsetters can set up to 24 point;
me can set up to 4 inches high.

stereo

SLANT

n the photosetter letters can be reversed, can
ve a screen over them, can be made to slope
ckwards or forwards, be elongated or
ntracted.

Author's corrections in hot metal are time-wasting, usually unnecessary or the result of incompetence and are inevitably costly. They are even more time-wasting and costly in photo-typesetting. It is important to send 'clean' copy to the printer and layouts should be accurate – really ACCURATE.

Modern typesetting machines produce a type-written proof which can be corrected before the film is made. Layouts for filmsetting should differ in one important particular from layouts for hot metal setting. There must be one line of reference, a base line, from which all measurements will be taken. For leading, indicate a measurement from the body line of one line of type to the body line of the next line.

Point
Sizes
X - HEIGHT
INTERLINEAR CHANNEL
X - HEIGHT
PT SIZE
PT SIZE

Display: Filmsetting offers various additional factors that are useful for design purposes. It is possible to lay a half-tone screen over letters to reduce their tone.

There are different types of filmsetters and it is advisable for the typographer to check with the printer for any peculiarities or limitations which he should follow. For display uses, some filmsetting machines can produce a letter 4″ high; most can set to 24 points.

Letters can be distorted.

There have been many articles in trade papers about photo-typesetting, but by far the simplest description that I have seen is in a little booklet called *Film Setting* issued by the Westerham Press in 1963, from which some of these illustrations have been reproduced.

a
u
t
o
b
louis
o
g
r
macniece
p
h
y

The principles of the acrostic can be effectively used, though this is not a true acrostic.

Before you start breaking rules, you should kno what they are. Once one knows what are the corre procedures one can look at them critically and se whether by deliberately flouting them anything ca be added to methods of communication. Certainl in advertising there is much to be said for unor thodox typography. A message has to be got across anything that helps may be justified, even if means using mixed-up founts, mutilating letters using punctuation marks from larger or smalle founts, turning words upside down . . .

There is even a place for illegibility. Playing abou with typefaces may result in a certain illegibility but may also result in a terrific visual excitemen All this has nothing, absolutely nothing to do wit the production of books where, I am very sure, an interference between author and reader is quit wrong. In fact dullness is infinitely preferable t oddity. The book page is not a medium for se expression. Nor for that matter, is any other kind typography. However eccentric the means he use the typographer is still only providing a medium communication between an author and a reader, or seller and a buyer. In the latter case it may be enoug if the buyer only registers in his mind the name the seller.

Media of communication outside printing ma condition the reflexes of our readers. T.V.screen and T.V. advertising have altered the appearan of much press advertising. Less and less is th ubiquitous man in the street inclined to read copy he is conditioned to looking at pictures and reading short, sharp, perhaps shocking headlines.

Advertisement for the magazine *Private Eye*, reminiscent of the dynamic typography of Russia and Germany in 1920's.

The possibilities for experimental typography are enormous. The few illustrations here give some indication of what can be done with type.

Cover for a typefounders booklet, designed by Hanns Lohrer. The original was printed in a solid green with the lettering in black and the apple in red. This striking design is made effective by its simplicity. The five letters of the word 'Foli provide the essential ingredients for the design; the apple may or may not have any special significance. 'An apple for the teacher', 'Eve's gift to Adam' . . .

British Railways booklet designed by Royston Cooper. The tumbling last letter of Broken Rail emphasises the sense of the line.

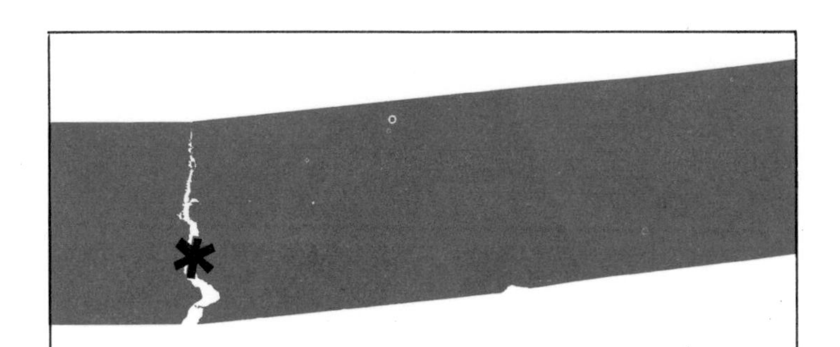

BROKEN RAIL

. . . Sounds really dramatic but is usually a simple fracture in a steel rail length.

450 tons at 80 m.p.h.

give the track a considerable thumping, and even a hairline crack can mean an unacceptably weak link in the Southern's 5,560 miles of track. The traditional lengthman's walking inspection–supplemented now by portable ultra-sonic flaw detectors–spots 83% of these while there is still time to deal with them during the quiet hours.

But there is still the unexpected serious breaks–and then the "Road-up" signs must go up while the one ton, 20-yard rail length is lifted and speedily replaced.

There are, as you may have guessed, quite a lot of other things that can go wrong. We do not want to depress you any further. And remember, Rolls Royces have been known to have punctures . . .

21

the inner

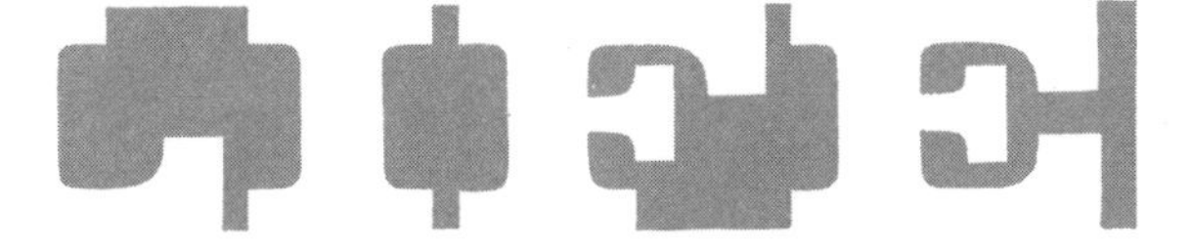

principle

'The Inner Life principle' from *ExperimentaTypographica II* by Dr Sandberg shows how type can be made readable by printing only the counters and the space between the letters. In this case there is also a double meaning.

*Verlag Galerie der Spiegel, Cologne*

come back early or never come

My father made the walls resound

He wore his collar dnuor yaw gnorw eht

Page from *Typographic Variations on the Poem Autobiography by Louis Macneice*. Designed as a typographic exercise by the students of the Plymouth College of Art.

A wall sheet showing some of the influences of the Industrial Revolution on letterforms in England. Designed by Stephen Abis, a first-year student at the Royal College of Art.

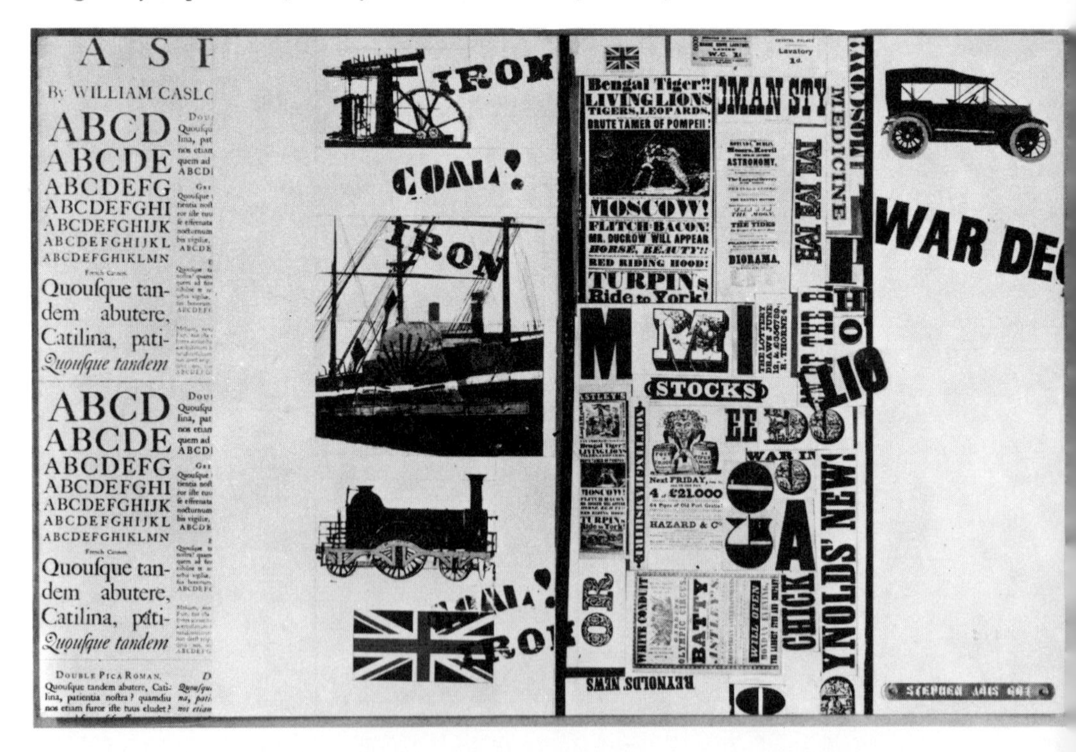

PHOTOGRAPH: OSBORNE

# BE AT BELMONT OCTOBER 1-27

*See the nation's best thoroughbreds battle for the big stakes at Belmont. Thrill to the heart-pounding action as they match strides in the $125,000 Champagne Stakes...in the $100,000 Jockey Club Gold Cup...in the $100,000 Man o' War...in nine big races each day, Monday through Saturday. Enjoy the beauty of Belmont, too. Luxurious restaurants, magnificent gardens, stately trees. Belmont is easy to reach: by car, on the Cross Island (Belt) Parkway; by special Long Island Rail Road trains from Penn Station direct to the track; or by subway and bus. First race 1:30. Be there!*

PREVIOUS PAGE
Advertisement from the *New Yorker* showing how the sense of movement in the picture is repeated in the italic typefaces used below.
It is worth noting that both these italic typefaces are sloping at the same angle.

Advertisement from the *New Yorker* for Underwood-Olivetti typewriters. The column of type serves as a support to the illustration.

The Underwood-Olivett
Studio 44 combines all the
advanced features and
sturdy dependability of a
full-size typewriter with the
lightness, beauty and com
pactness of a portable
That's why the Studio 44
is a favorite of student
and professional men the
world over...that's why i
makes such an excitin
gift, for anyone who write
at times and appreciate
beauty and excellence
Few other gifts that cos
so little provide so many
years of usefulness... few
others endure almost in
definitely as a happy re
minder of the giver.
You'll find the Studio 44
at all Underwood Portable
Dealers—and one of them
is not far from you. Ask
him to show you its many
features and exclusive
advantages. If you wish
he will also show you the
Underwood-Olivett
Lettera 22, a remarkably
complete ultra-lightweigh
portable typewriter, and
the Prima 20, a handsome
portable adding machine
that's winning favor for use
in the home. See him soon
Underwood Corporation
One Park Avenue, New
York 16, New York.
underwood


'The usefulness of jugs'. From *Experimenta Typographica II* by Dr Sandberg. Here there is a play on the sense of the word 'Kruges' (jugs), where the 'U' takes the form of a pitcher filled with water. It is a kind of rebus.
*Verlag Galerie der Spiegel, Cologne.*

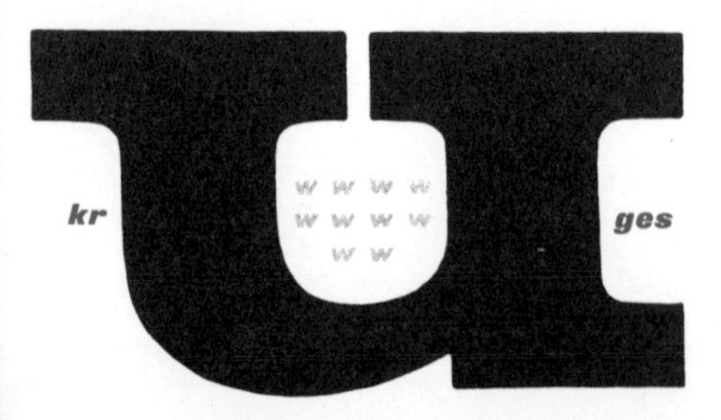

when i was 5 the BLACK DREAMS came

nothing after was quite the same

come back early or never come

Page from *Typographic Variations on the Poem Autobiography by Louis Macneice*. From the Plymouth College of Art. In the original, the type was printed in brown on a light brown paper, and the words 'Black Dreams' were for obvious reasons printed in black.

Front and back cover of a catalogue for the Stedelijk Museum, Amsterdam designed by Dr Sandberg.
The 'a' is the common factor in the title 'acht argentijnse abstracten'. The 'a' is printed in red on a brown board cover.

# CHAPTER V Notes on typographic styling

EMPHASIS

Originally, printers used roman, in contrast to th
black letter in use for normal text setting, for emphasis. Today there is a growing tendency to use a bol
face and sometimes a face unrelated to the tex
type; for example, in a setting in an old style typefac
the use of a bold sans serif. There are subtler way
of achieving this contrast, such as the use of
lighter than usual text type (such as Grot. 126) with
medium weight type for the bold (Monotype serie
215). Emphasis in text can also be achieved by th
use of italics, small capitals and on occasions b
underlining. This tends to be effective in large size
(above 30 pt), but it may be necessary to trim th
beard of the type, to bring the underlining close t
the body line.

HEADLINES

The larger the size of type you are using, the lighte
it can be; conversely the smaller the heading, th
bolder it needs to be. If you are using a secon
colour, always use a bolder face than you would i
you were using black only. For close setting of line
in capital letters, use titling capitals which have n
beard, so the foot of one letter can virtually rest o
the heads of the letters in the line below. In a serie
of lines of displayed copy, the sudden change fron
lower case to capitals for a single line can be effec
tive. Lines in capital letters tend to look lighter tha
those in lower case.

NUMERALS

There are two styles of numeral. Old style, 1234
67890 and modern or lining 1234567890. In tex
sizes (14 point and under) the old style numeral
will line up optically with lower case letters an
small capitals. The modern numerals will only lin

up with capitals. For display in larger sizes, the modern lining capitals are usually more effective. For copy with much figure work such as company reports etc, use lining capitals.

SPACING

The careful use of word-spacing, letter-spacing and punctuation marks can make a great difference to the appearance of the copy. Type for nearly all book and periodical work is set justified, that is with a straight edge down each side of the type matter. With lines of sixty or more characters, it is not difficult to set justified copy with visually even inter-word spacing. The normal inter-word spacing in any good Monotype house is 3 or 4 units (there are 18 units to an em of the body size). There is a long tradition behind this manner of close setting. It dates back to before printing began, when any scribe in a mediaeval monastery would ensure the evenness of his copy by his close spacing. To achieve this, he would resort to every kind of contraction and ligature. The printer's resources of contractions and ligatures are rather more limited but he can make use of some; he can also have a certain number of broken words at the end of a line, though he should avoid having broken words in more than two successive lines. The method of breaking words in appropriate places is discussed at length in the Oxford University Press's *Rules for Compositors and Readers*. The use of the ampersand '*&*' in the place of the word 'and' is just one permissible contraction to save a little space. Æ Œ, fi, ff, fl ffi ffl are some of the ligatures in normal use.

PUNCTUATION AND SPACES: for full points, colons and semicolons insert a hair space before the punctuation mark and normal inter-word spacing after. Commas should be set hard up to the preceding word.

QUOTATION MARKS: use single quotes in preference to double and do not set close up to the words they enclose but insert a hair space between the quote and the letter.

Setting punctuation marks outside the measure may cause the compositor some trouble, but can on occasions greatly improve the appearance of a piece of displayed setting.

'I pray God,' said Lord Hawke,
'that no professional will
ever captain England.' Poor Lord
Hawke!

Even in free setting, the single quotation mark looks better if thrown into the left margin.

There are endless refinements in the arrangement and spacing and placing of punctuation marks in displayed setting. For further information on spacing, consult Geoffrey Dowding's book *Finer Points in the Spacing and Arrangement of Type* (Wace).

NARROW MEASURES: Practically the only method of achieving even spacing in narrow columns of type of less than 30 characters is by free setting, that is with a straight left hand edge and a ragged right hand edge, as results when typewriting. This is rather more difficult to set because the lines as far as possible should be broken as the sense dictates. For narrow measures always use a small setting. The wider the measure the larger the type.

LETTER-SPACING IN DISPLAY: Any capitals larger than 8 point look better with letter-spacing, with the sole exception of condensed capitals, which are designed as space-savers and if spaced at all widely not only lose their purpose but also tend to look like a row of fencing posts and become unreadable.

Condensed type should be set solid, whether the words are set in capitals or small letters.

**PRINTED Ephemera**

**P R I N T E D**
**E p h e m e r a**

L A N D I N G - S T A G E     LANDING-STAGE

Too great a letter-spacing (left) makes copy more difficult to read. The juxtaposition of the capital letters 'L' and 'A' governs the letter-spacing through the rest of the copy.

.ANDING STAGE
VOODBRIDGE

.ANDING STAGE

VOODBRIDGE

'op: Too much space between the words
ANDING and STAGE and too little space
etween the lines. Below: a reasonable spacing.

The amount of letter-spacing used for capital letters should be about the same as the space between the verticals of a capital letter 'H' of the fount. Letters must be visually, not mechanically spaced.

Never letter-space or word-space for that matter, to more than the space between the lines. Trust your eye more than any mechanical method of positioning your spacing.

In display, though lower case letters are used very widely there are still certain occasions when capitals look better. For instance in headlines on title pages of books or for very short words which, when set in lower case, may make an awkward shape; words such as bag BAG, pal PAL, ape APE.

bag BAG pal PAL ape APE

ALIGNMENT

When displaying capital letters, where more than one line has to line up vertically with another, the letters A C G J O G Q S T V W X Y should be lined up optically; that is, they should over run the measure. The most difficult capital letter to begin or end a line with is T with its over hanging cross bar. The word 'THE' is one of the most difficult words to space and position.

'ertical alignment of difficult letters. The 'N'
f Normandy ranges with the left margin,
ıe 'A' and 'T' are thrown out slightly.

THE

ARCHITECTURE OF

NORMANDY

PUNCTUATION

With punctuation marks, a more even effect can be achieved if certain marks such as hyphens, full points, commas and quotes are also thrown out beyond the measure (cf. Gutenberg Bible). On the other hand it is better to keep exclamation and interrogation marks, colons and semicolons within the type area as these are of a similar weight to normal lower case letters.

# CONTROL?

The use for emphasis of question and exclamation marks from different founts

# We have told you how good we are!

REFINEMENTS IN DISPLAY SETTING

Certain founts of type suffer from defects such as having over heavy punctuation marks. It may be worth while on occasions substituting punctuation marks from a different fount, where they are lighter or narrower. There may be times when typematter is to be reproduced photographically where one can re-draw awkward or ill-shaped characters.

sea-green SEA-GREEN SEA-GREEN

Hyphens, correctly cast for lower case (left) are too low for capitals (centre) so have them cast higher on the body of the type (right).

(sea-green) (SEA-GREEN) (SEA-GREEN)

Parentheses, correctly cast for lower case (left) are too low for capitals (centre) so have them cast higher on the body of the type (right).

Hyphens and dashes normally centre on the x-height of the lower case letters; if set with capitals, they must be cast higher on the body. The same suggestion should be applied to brackets [ ] and parentheses ( ) which are designed for lower case and look sadly out of place with capitals.

## PARAGRAPH BREAKS

In text setting, to relieve monotony, or to indicate a new train of thought, copy is set in paragraphs. The beginning of a new paragraph is usually indicated by an indentation of an em of the body size. Copy is usually set full out at the beginning of a chapter or under a subheading. Some printers and typographers prefer to set the first line of all paragraphs full out. In that case, to indicate the end of a paragraph insert a white line. The insertion of a lead makes backing up impossible.

Another way to indicate the beginning of a new paragraph is to throw the first line out 12 points or so into the margin. This can be effective, and is used with some success in certain daily newspapers. The scribe's method of running copy on but dividing paragraphs with special paragraph marks is effective enough in black letter setting but I have rarely seen it done with any success for roman typefaces.

**Having written those rash words we touch wood, cross our fingers and throw salt over the shoulder, to propitiate the malevolent gods waiting to stamp out any spark of optimism in a nuclear world.**

**But this time the chances do seem good. For five years Britain, America and Russia have been immersed in Geneva talks aiming at an agreement to explode no more nuclear devices, but never reaching it.**

**There have been seasons of hope and despair, encouragement and disappointment, promise and betrayal.**

The Comment Column from the London *Daily Mail.*

**AS towchyng the comyng of our lord in our bodyly flessh, we may considre thre thynges of this comyng. That is to wete thoportunyte, the necessyte & the vtylyte ¶ The oportunyte of comyng is taken by the reson of the man that first was vanquysshyd in the lawe of nature of the default of the knowledge of god, by whiche he fyll in to euyll errours, & therfore he was constrayned to crye to god ¶ Illumina oculos meos, that is to saye, lord gyue lyght to myn eyen. After cam the lawe of god whiche hath gyuen commandement in which he hath ben overcome of Impuissance, as first he hath cryed ther is non that fulfilleth, but that comandeth. For ther he is only**

The use of paragraph marks by William Morris to save starting the paragraph on a new line.

Title-page designed by Jan Tschichold for his *Designing Books*.

*JAN TSCHICHOLD*

DESIGNING BOOKS

*Planning a book*
*A typographer's composition rules*
*Fifty-eight examples*
*by the author*

Wittenborn, Schultz, Inc.
New York

BOOK DESIGN AND PRODUCTION

From the time of the great fifteenth century Ven tian printers such as the brothers J. and W. d Spira, Nicholas Jenson and Aldus Manutius, th form, shape and margins of the book page have nc altered much. At last there are signs of a litt loosening up and the classical margins, agreeab though they are, are not the only margins one ca usefully use in a book. For a book that is to be hel in the hand and read, the classical margins st provide what is probably the best solution.[7] Fc illustrated books, for books of instruction, for boo with tabular matter there are possible alternative Certainly for many reference books, an asymmetr

7. *Designing Books:* Jan Tschichold. Wittenborn, Schultz. Inc. New York.

page arrangement, with the wide margin appearing always to the left (or right) of the type may be a more useful arrangement. And with typographic skill it need not look outlandish, though it may cause difficulty in imposition.

For traditional books (and traditional is not to be taken as a slighting term) printed on antique paper, which is a paper with a soft surface, 'old face' types are ideal, typefaces such as Bembo, Caslon, Garamond, Fournier. For smooth or art papers it is usually better to use a typeface with a greater inking surface, such as Baskerville, Plantin, Times New Roman, Ehrhardt, the Ionics and the Moderns, Walbaum, Caledonia, Bulmer, though Walbaum can look well on softer papers.

In book production, an important typographic factor is the set, or the relative width of the lower case alphabet. There are occasions when one wants to bulk out a book, and so uses a typeface with a wide set such as Baskerville, Imprint, Modern Extended, or Old Style. For narrow setting, Bembo, Fournier, Ehrhardt are all economical of space. Space saving can also be achieved by setting in a smaller size of typeface with a large x-height such as Plantin, Times New Roman or Scotch Roman which are the optical equivalent of, up to two sizes larger, a long ascender

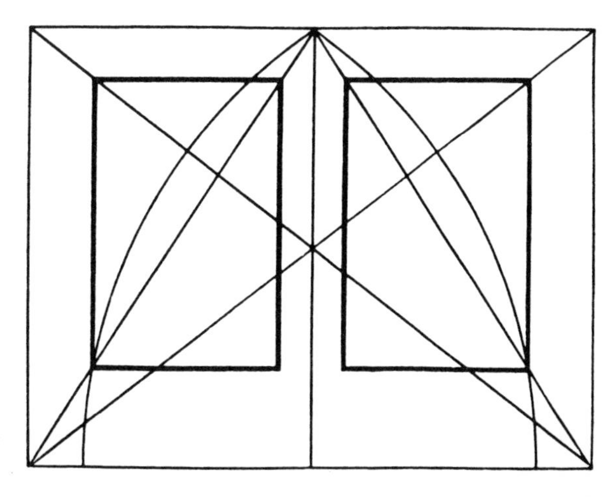

Classical proportions for page margins from Jan Tschichold's *Designing Books*.

and descender type (9 point Times visually equa
11 point Bembo). The use of grotesques for boo
work is increasing. They are best set in small size
in light weights and to narrow measures. They a
not as flexible as seriffed letters, having no sma
capitals, and usually ill-favoured italics.

In laying out a book there are certain convention
such as the order for the preliminary pages.[8] The
conventions can be a useful guide, but I would n
hesitate to break them. The sequence is usual
something like this:

| page | | |
|---|---|---|
| 1 | Half title | The text of the book wi begin on the right han page facing either a blan page, or the last page the Introduction |
| 2 | Blank or could be frontispiece | |
| 3 | Title page | |
| 4 | Imprint, date of publication, setting particulars, copyright details | Errata, printed on a separate slip will be tipped-in opposite the first page of the next |
| 5 | Dedication* | |
| 6 | Blank | |
| 7 | Acknowledgements* | At the end of the boo will come any addition matter, such as Appendi Author's notes, Glossar Bibliography and, lastl Index |
| 8 | Blank | |
| 9 | Contents | |
| 10 | Blank | |
| 11 | List of illustrations* | |
| 12 | Blank | |
| 13 | Preface* | |
| 14 | Blank | |
| 15 | Introduction* | |

* These of course may not be present

Another convention is the running headline. T
usual convention is: title of book on left hand pag
title of chapter or subject of page on right han
Folios can be incorporated in the running hea
Omit these in pocket size books or in books wi

8. *Introduction to Typography:* Oliver Simon. Penguin Books, Harmondsworth.

many subheadings. They are usually set in text size small capitals.

The typographer working on book production has two other problems: the lettering on the case of a book and the book jacket. The latter is a problem widely removed from the text pages of a book. It is a graphic design problem of marketing. There is no need to use the same faces on the jacket, not even for the blurbs on the flaps that turn over inside the book. In fact, if the text of the book is printed on an antique paper and the jacket has a smooth surface, it would be a mistake. For blurbs, which are rarely more than 14 ems measure, use a narrow set typeface, such as Ehrhardt.

For the brasses of a book, use typefaces that are not too heavy, that are without hairlines and, most important, that have large counters that will not fill in, such as Plantin or Ionic.

The gap between the design of books and the design of periodicals has narrowed markedly in the last few years. A typographer's job is after all, communication and if certain methods of layout help to put over ideas more effectively than others, then they are just as valid for books as they are for periodicals or advertising. Advertising design in periodicals, used to be more lively than the editorial matter, both in copy and in presentation. Today the editorial layout is frequently more exciting than the advertising.

Ninety per cent of a typographer's job in periodical work is of course the layout and general presentation. It is just another graphic design job. There are, however, certain points that should be watched.

PROCESS

This conditions the choice of types for text-setting. For letterpress on coated papers use types with a good inking surface, such as Times New Roman. For stereo use medium weight types, without hair lines, such as Ionic or Imprint. For offset, use lighter weight types, but avoid hairlines. Types such as

Baskerville. For gravure, which mutilates and also thickens any typeface, use a light weight face such as Old Style.

Type for half-tones. The procedure for this is the same for any process and merely means providing the blockmaker or reproduction studio with type pulls on Baryta paper, indicating whether the type matter is to appear in black or in white (i.e. in reverse) in the dark areas of a half-tone. This is then put to camera and stripped into the negative (or positive) used for block or plate.

Lithographed letterheading for a Belgian restaurant c. 1820.

## THE DESIGN OF STATIONERY

Letterheads and billheads are often the first image a potential customer may receive from a company or a professional man. They are clearly of very great importance. The letterhead should not only be clear and readable, but should reflect something of the character of the sender. A jobbing printer who is expert at colour work needs a very different heading from one of the University Presses. This should be fairly obvious; I will not labour the point, except to say that a dogmatic design approach can produce very unsuitable pieces of printing.

I doubt if there is any greater justification for using an asymmetric layout than a symmetric one. Both can be effective. Dignity is certainly most easily achieved by symmetry; flexibility and informality by asymmetry.

Lithographed heading for a French biscuit manufacturer 1838.
Modern engraved headings can be lithographed or die-stamped.

THE HISTORICAL SOCIETY OF PENNSYLVANIA

*Founded 1824*

1300 Locust Street · Philadelphia 7, Pa.

Letterheading for a Historical Society set in Caslon Old Face.

Westerham Press Limited
High Street Westerham Kent

Telephone 2256/3312
Telex 8870
Telegrams
Print Westerham Telex

Directors
R. S. Atterbury
Max Rayne

Printer's letterheading set in Grotesque 215.

**der direktor**

hochschule für gestaltung

**bauhaus dessau**

**postanschrift: bauhaus dessau**

fernruf: sammel-nr. 3136, nach geschäftsschluß: **1587**
bankkonto: städtische kreissparkasse dessau nr. **2634**
postscheck: magdeburg 13701

ihre zeichen ihre nachricht vom unsere zeichen tag

Letterhead for the Bauhaus Dessau (1930) set in Aurora grotesque

---

**Max Ebel & Sohn** **Baustoffhandel**

**Mainz-Weisenau**

Fernruf Sammelnummer 43206
Telegramme ebelbau mainz
Lager: Mainz-Weisenau, Rheinstraße

Datum

**RECHNUNG**

Wir sandten Ihnen auf Ihre Rechnung und Gefahr

Letterheading for builder's merchant from the Bauer Typefoundry, Frankfurt-am-Main, set in Folio grotesque

**STENDIG** **incorporated** / imported furniture / **600 madison avenue** / **new york city 22** / **telephone: eldorado 5·1460**

Furniture importer's letterheading, with the name in an outline Egyptian and the rest of the copy in Berthold grotesque.

---

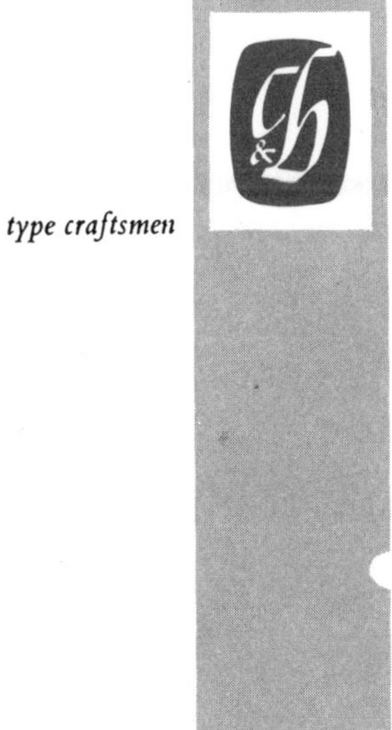

*type craftsmen*

COOPER & BEATTY, LIMITED

*401 Wellington West at Spadina, Toronto 2B, Canada · Phone Empire 4-7272*

Typesetter's letterheading set in Bembo and Bembo Italic, with a blind-blocking of a piece of type.

---

Percy Lund Humphries & Co Ltd 12 Bedford Square WC1

**Lund Humphries**

London
**Telephone: Museum 7676 Telegrams: Lund Museum 7676**
Bradford
**The Country Press**
**Telephone: 41311·2·3 Telegrams: Typography Bradford**

Printers

Binders

Publishers

Printer's letterheading set in Baskerville and a grotesque.

PAPER SIZES

British paper sizes are a very true manifestation of the Anglo-Saxon genius for illogicallity! They bear little relation to one another and have a host of curious names such as post, large post, small post, pinched post etc. There was clearly need for new thinking, and the adoption by British Standards in 1960 of the International Paper sizes has produced a series of sizes based on logical geometric progression. There are three series of international sizes, designated A, B and C. For the purpose of this discussion on stationery, we will only consider the A series. The basis of the A size is a rectangle 1 square metre with sides in proportion 1 : $\sqrt{2}$. This means that the long side is 1189 mm and the short 841 mm. If the shorter side is doubled or the longer side halved, that is, if the sheet is doubled or halved, the sides are still in the same proportion. The trimmed sizes of the A series are as follows:

| Designation | Millimetres | Inches |
|---|---|---|
| 2A | 1189 × 1682 | 46.81 × 66.22 |
| A0 | 841 × 1189 | 33.11 × 46.81 |
| A1 | 594 × 841 | 23.39 × 33.11 |
| A2 | 420 × 594 | 16.54 × 23.39 |
| A3 | 297 × 420 | 11.69 × 16.54 |
| A4 | 210 × 297 | 8.27 × 11.69 |
| A5 | 148 × 210 | 5.83 × 8.27 |
| A6 | 105 × 148 | 4.13 × 5.83 |
| A7 | 74 × 105 | 2.91 × 4.13 |

The most useful size for business letters is A4 (8.27 × 11.69″) and for professional correspondence A5 (5.83 × 11.69″). Having said all this there are still many people who prefer the old large post 'quarto' and 'octavo' sizes of 10″ × 8″ and 8″ × 5″.

Having established the paper size or sizes, it is most important to scale your heading to the paper size. A setting that looks well on a quarto sheet may look over large on an octavo sheet, particularly if printed the narrow way of the sheet. (The long way, is of course the same size as the width of the quarto sheet). There is much to be said for simplicity. It is possible to set the whole of a professional heading in one size. If emphasis is needed for any part, this can be set in the same size in a bolder face or in a different colour. There is no dogmatic reason for keeping to the same size. It does simplify setting but this point, I think, has been over laboured by the purists. It is also in some ways easier and gives a more even tone. For many kinds of letterheads, it may be necessary to make much more of the name block so, though the rest of the letterhead is set in one size, the company name could appear much larger, and possibly in a different colour.

Apart from these general observations on design, there is the all important matter of detail, and minute detail at that. The care over detail is a typographic necessity in any printed work; in small jobs like letterheads it is of overwhelming importance. There is so little to see in a letterhead anyway, that everything should be exact and precise. A punctuation mark ill-placed can look disastrous . . .

PUNCTUATION

In good text setting, unnecessary punctuation is omitted in order to help close, even setting. The same applies to letterheads. For instance omit full points after Ltd, Mr, Mrs, Dr (for Doctor but not after Dr. for Debtor as on a billhead).

In postal addresses, insert full points after the letters but not after the numeral (so W.C.1 or N.W.3); letters representing degrees, decorations etc. can be set either with or without full points, thus: C B E, R D I or C.B.E., R.D.I. but M.A., D. Litt. or M.A., Ph.D. If there is any possible ambiguity or humorous interpretation such as B U M P for British Union of Master Printers, use full points. This applies to the use of punctuation anywhere.

Omit commas after street or road numbers: 55 East 57th Street; and between city and postal districts: New York 22. Authorities do not agree on many of these *minutiae*. These suggestions are made to give you a point of departure.

When using capital letters, in sizes above 8 point, letter-space optically. This means marking up your layout with the exact amount of space needed. When using numerals for telephone numbers etc. use capitals with modern (or ranging) figures, small capitals with old style figures. On the whole, ranging figures are better for stationery.

If a date has to be printed in full, the most satisfactory method is 11 December 1912 or 11 : 12 : 1912. The latter can cause confusion, for though it is understandable to an English reader, an American letter writer puts the month down first, then the day, so December 11, 1912 or 12: 11: 1912. For further observations on the layout of stationery, see Herbert Spencer's book *Design in Business Printing* (Sylvan Press); for further notes on punctuation see *Rules for Compositors and Readers* (Oxford).

CONCLUSION

Typography is to me a subject of unending interest Its ramifications are so wide. Its successful practice depends on many things; it depends on an understanding of the meaning of words, on a knowledge of printing processes, and on a meticulous attention to detail. I think also, that it depends on the typographer being a cultured man, that is, someone who is conscious of both the past and the present in the arts, in literature and in the crafts of printing and typography[9]. This knowledge is not mere scholarly pedantry, but something that makes one alive to the fact that typographic design is as fluid as language and as changing as modern life.

9. M. Michel Saint-Denis addressing the Royal College af Art on a similar theme on 12 July 1963 said; ". . . by a cultured man, I don't mean one who is polite." Nor do I.

| | |
|---|---|
| AMPERSAND | Contraction of 'and' & |
| ANTIQUE PAPER | Good quality paper with a rough surface. |
| ART PAPER | Clay-coated paper with a shiny surface. |
| ASCENDER | The part of the letter that is above the x-height, l, h, etc. |
| BACKING-UP | Printing the reverse of a sheet with the lines exactly lining up with those on the other side. |
| BANK PAPER | Thin, tough almost transparent paper suitable for layout work. |
| BARYTA PAPER | A coated paper, used for reproduction proofs. |
| BEARD | The metal sloping away from the face of a letter, at head or foot. Can be trimmed to allow for closer spacing between lines. |
| BLACK LETTER | Gothic or 'old English' typeface. |
| BODY | The solid shank of the letter. |
| BODY LINE | The line at the foot of a lower case letter x. |
| BOLTS | The folded edges of the printed sheet at head, tail and fore-edge before trimming. |
| BRASSES | A deeply cut brass block, specially for blocking on bindings. |
| BROADSHEET | Large sheet of paper usually printed on one side only. |
| CASTING-OFF | Assessing the length of a manuscript to estimate the number of pages of a given size of type. |
| DESCENDER | The part of the type below the x-height. |
| FOLIO | Page number. |
| FRAKTUR | In Germany the name given to gothic (or black letter) typefaces. |
| FULL POINT | Printer's term for full stop. |
| GRAVURE | A method of intaglio printing from flat or rotary plates. |
| HALF-TONE | Printing plate of copper or zinc, photographically produced. |
| HOT METAL | Letterpress printing as opposed to filmsetting. |
| IMPOSITION | The arrangement of pages in position for printing, governing the correct sequence when folded. |

| | |
|---|---|
| INSERT | Sheet or part of a sheet placed inside another shee after folding, to complete the sequence of paginatior of a section. |
| JUSTIFIED SETTING | The equal and exact spacing of letters and words tc a given measure. |
| LEADING | Strips of lead less than type height, used for spacing out lines of type. |
| LETTERPRESS | Printing from raised blocks or type. |
| LIGATURE | Tied letters such as ffi ffl cast on one body to save space and damage to the kerns. |
| LINING NUMERALS | Numerals all the same height as the capital letters |
| L.C. | Lower case or small letters. |
| OFFSET PRINTING | Printing from a lithographic stone or plate transfer- red by a rubber roller to the paper. |
| OLD STYLE NUMERALS | Numerals with ascenders and descenders. |
| PICA EM | Approx. 1/6th of an inch, a twelve point em (Ameri- can point system). |
| QUADRAT | Pieces of blank metal less than type height used tc fill spaces and short lines in a page of type. |
| RUN ON | A sentence continued in the same line as the pre- vious one, not a distinct paragraph. Chapters start- ing below the previous one on the same page are said to run on. |
| RUNNING HEAD | The heading at the top of a page. |
| SERIES NUMBER | All Monotype faces have series numbers. |
| STEREO | A replica from type or block cast in metal from a papier maché mould. |
| STONE | The large table in a composing room where formes of type are assembled within the chase. |
| SUPERIOR FIGURE | Small letter or figure cast on the shoulder of a sor to print above the x-height of the preceding letter |
| TIP-IN | An illustration or other loose plate pasted in at its back margin. |
| WHITE LINE | The space exactly the depth of a line of type, pu between lines, to make a space that will not interfere with exact backing up. |
| WRAP-ROUND | Pages of illustrations wrapped round a section, o part of a section, in the make-up of a book. |
| X-HEIGHT | The height of the main body of a piece of type, no counting ascenders or descenders. |